WHAT READERS ARE SAYING ABOUT FOR GOODNESS' SAKE

All people want a purpose, and all organizations should want one as well. *For Goodness' Sake* takes us on a compelling and inspiring journey showing us how organizations can do well and do good, and why they must do both.

Rahul Bhardwaj
President & CEO, Institute of Corporate Directors

Chris Houston offers a compelling alternative to the idea of a corporation as a gathering mechanism where better is defined as more. *For Goodness' Sake* declares that business can be about living out of a purpose-for-others, in service to society. The proposals are clear and the implications are game changing.

Roger Laing
Vice President and Business Unit Leader, RLG International
Board Chair, Regent College

A clear, helpful guide that brings both understanding to where we are and insight into how each of us individually and collectively can help create positive change. I highly recommend *For Goodness' Sake*.

Katie Archdekin
Consultant, entrepreneur & former bank executive

I'm so glad that work like this is being published.

Grant Tudor
Social innovator – Founder & CEO, Populist

This book makes me think there could be hope... now the big challenge is getting this book into the hands of as many business leaders as possible.

Julia Hall
Account Executive, Risk Management Solutions

The writing is simply beautiful, meaningful, and captured my heart and mind… it captures everything I've always felt intuitively about the organization I worked for – a love hate relationship that I could never reconcile. It gives hope and inspiration that we can change things for the better. I hope this book gets the attention it deserves.

Wendy Tite
Retired bank executive

For Goodness' Sake is not a typical business book. It is something much more like a call to revolution. It disturbs, inspires, challenges, and invites us to aspire to a form of business that is higher, purer, holier, and more powerful.

Chris Wignall
Executive Director, The Catalyst Foundation

I thought I would take a break from what I was doing to read just the first few pages, but it hooked me and took me on a journey… into a world of telos and true deep intent of a life in service with others… a great read!

Don Jones
Founder & Chief Experience Designer, Exper!ence It Inc.

NO ONE is as capable of synthesizing the broad experience of working with leading executives and companies, combining the experience with brilliant and relevant insights and then with remarkable creativity showing us the way to a new form of successful business organization. Read Chris Houston's ideas on Telosity and join the action to make it happen!

Dr. Joe DiStefano
Professor Emeritus, IMD (Lausanne, Switzerland)
Professor Emeritus, Richard Ivey School of Business (University of Western Ontario)

For Goodness' Sake: Satisfy the hunger for meaningful business

Chris Houston

With

Jordan Pinches

Editor: *Jeremy Katz*
Copy editors: *Robert M. Graff, Gail Patejunas*
Creative director: *Gabe Usadel*
Art directors: *Connor Fleming, Lucia Vaughan*
Illustration: *Lucia Vaughan*
Design: *Ogilvy 485 Branding & Graphic Design*
Cover design: *Brian Liu*

ISBN 978-0-9959824-0-6 (paperback)
ISBN 978-0-9959824-2-0 (hardcover)
ISBN 978-0-9959824-1-3 (epub)

Typeface: *Ogilvy J Baskerville & Baskerville*

For Jeannie

56 The character of every purposeful enterprise

66 How to bring a purposeful enterprise to life

82 A purposeful enterprise starts with you

INTRODUCTION

Sometimes, and usually without the intention to shape history, important people say things that echo through the ages because they signal the rise and fall of eras in human history. Often they seem rather inane at the time, and only later, with the benefit of hindsight, do we see them as pivotal or recognize that they have summed up the close of an era or the birth of a new one.

One such moment happened in 2007, on the precipice of the financial crisis, when Citigroup CEO Chuck Prince summed up his company's attitude for the present and plan for the future by saying, "As long as the music is playing, you've got to get up and dance. We're still dancing." That was the "last call" that rang out from the bar at the economic party that had been raging since the Industrial Revolution.

Today, the music has stopped.

Our tragedy of the commons

We have designed businesses that are ruthlessly efficient at the one and only thing we have asked them to do: apply the very primitive rules of economic rationalism to the task of wealth creation with little regard for anything else. Sure, we have put up a few regulatory fences so they don't run entirely amok, but we really only ask this entity called a "business" to do one thing well — make money.

It hasn't always been this way. In the medieval English village, built around a shared green commons used for grazing animals, it was always in the interest of each villager to add just one more sheep to his flock, until the habitat was overgrazed and transformed into a dry, hardened patch of dirt and the whole system collapsed, seemingly overnight, and served no one. Such thresholds exist today, and there are many "commons" which are either reaching their limits or already in precipitous decline. All the profit-seeking we have been doing has come at an astronomical price, which we are now being forced to reconcile.

The point is, whether it's management of flocks or economic systems, there is a "music stops" moment for every complex system that is demanded to yield a single variable.

If we had known how to look, we might have seen this coming. Thankfully, our tragedy of the commons is not complete. It's not too late … yet. We must act now and act wisely.

The panarchy principle

If we had understood a principle of complex systems called *panarchy* when we were designing our businesses, we would have chosen a set of aims more diverse than simple profit-taking.

Panarchy

A natural law governing complex systems, from which we can infer that a system which is managed to optimize a single variable may produce the desired result for a time. But that result will be compromised over the long term as the greater complexity of the system is revealed. Single-variable optimization eventually destabilizes the whole system, introducing an unpredictable entropy. The system, no longer resilient, degrades (often with shocking speed) into a radically new state. From such disorder, new forms arise.

There are signs everywhere that *panarchy* is baked into the way our world works. Consider the well-known but often complex ecosystem of a person's life, which, it would seem, gives evidence for the veracity of this natural law.

We need look no further than the workaholic who has maximized the variable of career above all other pursuits and relationships. That single-variable optimization will eventually have consequences resulting in some unique combination of fraying family and relationships, degrading personal health and wellness, mental and emotional exhaustion, and over time, the feeling that collapse is imminent unless balance can be restored — at the very least through a decent vacation, but often a job or career change, a sabbatical, or some other extended hiatus.

Predictably, some of the most noticeable signs of the applicability of *panarchy* turn up in nature.

When a fisher finds a good trout stream, she doesn't throw a net across the mouth of the river so she can catch every trout in the system right then and there. Doing so would provide her an immediate wealth of fish (and maybe make her the talk of the town), but it would also compromise the trout population of that stream — a real negative if she wants to continue as a successful fisher of trout. That is the obvious effect.

A less obvious effect would occur the following spring (and every spring thereafter) in the form of unintended consequences. When a large number of trout are no longer part of the complex ecosystem, it spurs a population boom of both mayflies and caddis flies, which used to be kept in check as the trout ate masses of larvae hatching every spring in the calmer sections of the waterway. Of course, a plague of pesky bugs is only one unintended consequence among many imbalances that spread across the system, introducing new ones further afield, affecting its members in complex ways, and creating new norms. The bonanza yield is no longer possible. Or, if the system is able to maintain near-peak capacity for a time but growth is the expectation, last year's bonanza becomes inadequate.

Our global regulation of fisheries and other complex ecosystems, imperfect though it may be, is a direct result of learning about *panarchy* the hard way.

It's a lesson that we as a species are slow to grasp, particularly when we have to value the future as highly as the present. For the past couple of centuries, we have set up commerce and our complex economic systems to optimize the single variable of profit, acting as though *panarchy* didn't exist. Natural laws do not tolerate being contravened indefinitely. The consequences of the past hundred-plus years of management are becoming more apparent and may soon become irreversible. Our economy feels a bit like a volatile, quivering mess. We have a rash of bankruptcies and defaults, scarce prospects for growth, and an impending climatological disaster.

THE FAILURE OF SUCCESS
(AND HOW WE GOT HERE)

Over the past couple of centuries, human society has seen perhaps the most rapid change and tumultuous cultural and social shifts we have ever known. It is important to understand some of those key changes because they have shaped us and the world we know.

The period historians call the Enlightenment (late 1500s to early 1800s) is no doubt the "granddaddy of the modern age." In addition to forming three pillars of Western Civilization today (capitalism, democracy, and industrialization), the Enlightenment also set in motion two less obvious but equally notable shifts. These are changes that have taken place under the surface, in the personal and social psyche. In many ways, these movements are even more monumental because they are shifts in belief, thought, and, ultimately, our understanding of human identity.

The advent of the free-market economy — predicated on competition, self-interest, and systemized borrowing and investment — marked the start of capitalism's climb and the ascendancy of free-market economics. That, in turn, allowed flexibility and nimble response and promoted scale and innovation. But, from its early days, capitalism was also founded on the generally accepted theory that economic growth is based on consumption and production, and therefore, personal spending (or debt) and consumerism are necessary for growth and wealth creation. The corporation arose as a method of business organization and a vehicle for growing, directing, and protecting shared wealth.

With the proliferation of industrialization and mechanization, and the exponential growth in new applications of technology, the way we interacted with our natural surroundings and the way we organized work were monumentally changed. Suddenly, we could use natural resources in fascinating and productive ways — and consume and waste them at lightning speed. We created modern management techniques, professionalization, and division of labor, thereby spawning highly complex production systems with the goal of organizing people and processes in order to provide the necessary support structure for a staggering degree of manufacturing complexity.

Seizing back power from a rational ruler

The *age of reason* that was the Enlightenment spurred technical advances and better tools, an increasingly literate population, and the first stages of globalization – colonialism, really – as our ability to study life and learn about its complexities grew rapidly. The more we learned, the more we desired to gain intellectual and scientific understanding about everything in the natural world.

Heliocentrism, new biological and medical discoveries, the study of gravity, the discipline of chemistry … the list could go on. Our understanding of the world was being turned inside out, quite literally.

This rise of rationalism – and, in particular, the scientific method of gathering information through a hypothetico-deductive system of observation, hypothesis formation, and experimentation – presented a fact-based way of reaching a conclusion about reality. Rationalism, which began as one way of knowing and understanding reality alongside philosophy and theology, had by the mid-20th century become the only way to know anything with certainty. The hegemony of science was begun, and before this epistemological juggernaut, all mystery evaporates. Thus the installation of a rational ruler to govern the Western way of thinking was underway.

We have theorized and calculated scientific conclusions about the nature of reality, and now we also analyze just about every other aspect of the human experience. This scientization and rationalization of everything has of course extended into business, especially the study of management. The rationalist mindset has given us things like modern management techniques and mathematical economic models and theories to govern the complex human interactions that compose business. But most notably, the rise of rationalism fused with the scientific examination of economic interactions to create a preference for choices and actions that were economically rational and, above all, made financial sense.

Today, economic justification rules the roost, which has made central bankers, industry barons, stockbrokers, and prognosticating economists the great oracles and power brokers of commerce. Making money has become an irrefutable logic — and in business we give it ultimate deference.

Our preference for rationalism led us to insist that we could, through scientific study, gain mastery of all aspects of our world, even the economy. However, economic rationalism has its limits: No amount of understanding will grant us the ability to foresee the unexpected or to master all the great mysteries of the universe or to predict unfailingly the way a complex financial system will respond to our mercurial participation. Though mathematical and scientific leaps and bounds have been rapid and remarkable, there is still much that remains unknowable and, ultimately, beyond our control — and mercifully, much that always
will remain so.

Despite our culture's deference for economic rationalism, we balance it in our own lives against other sensibilities quite regularly. For instance, it makes little economic sense for me to leave my office and take a walk through the sugar bush on my farm when a client has come to me for help with an urgent and vexing problem. I could certainly bill more hours sitting at my desk, but getting out in nature helps me think more clearly and creatively, so I often take this time.

The point in the end is a simple one: We are not machines subject only to logical frameworks and rationalist rules. Rather, we are multifaceted beings who rely on a wide range of inputs and sensibilities to make choices. Yet in recent decades, especially in the Western world, we have adopted a method of corporate decision-making that is almost entirely economically rationalist. Given the uneasy state of our present systems of commerce and governance, it's time to question the validity of that approach.

Rationalism is no doubt a trusted companion for our human experience and our management of business, but it is not appropriate for economic rationalism to be the mode of thinking and decision-making that rules all others. Should we continue to give it such power of influence?

The individual revolution continues

In recent centuries, as we created and evolved our systems of commerce and governance, and we grew to understand ourselves and our humanity more deeply, fundamental human questions remained. How do we understand ourselves in relation to one another? What are our roles within this new system and in society? We can look to the Ancients for answers. Ultimately, we are each asking, "Who am I?" In Latin, the Romans had two words, *ipse* and *idem,* to help frame their understanding of the self.

Ipse refers to a self that is unique, self-defined, and independent. Ipse says, "I am me, myself; I am an individual."

Idem refers to a self that is literally "the same as." Idem is the self, defined in the context of others. Idem says, "I am with you; part of us; in relationship to; I am a person."

Both *ipse* and *idem,* obviously, pronounce essential aspects of our human identity, and the human condition compels us to embrace each in tension — our own uniqueness in relationship to others. However, much of human history has been shaped by the oscillation of preference for one or the other.

Indeed, for nearly two millennia, our forebears answered the existential questions of what it means to be a person in relationship to the divine, but then René Descartes, a French mathematician writing 400 years ago, coined a phrase that eventually changed the course of Western civilization, setting it on a path to the present. *Cogito ergo sum* — "I think, therefore I am" — became the foundational concept of a thought revolution.

Other writers such as John Locke, whose theories suggested self-definition, as in "I am who I perceive myself to be," and Nietzsche, whose concept of the *übermensch* (a classification he believed he exemplified) went beyond self-definition to ascribe almost divine status to the individual, saying, "I am the heroic great man: new, unique, incomparable, self-defined." Needless to say, this only fed the growing torrent of individual independence. And then there was Adam Smith, whose most famous ideas on economics and the "invisible hand" — the indiscernible agent that guides a free market to supply-demand

equilibrium – only slightly overshadowed his affirmation of self-interest and the right to private property. It was he, after all, who wrote, "It is not from the benevolence of the butcher, the brewer, or the baker, that we expect our dinner, but from their regard to their own interest. We address ourselves, not to their humanity but to their self-love, and never talk to them of our own necessities but of their advantages."

There have been competing voices, of course. In the 1800s, for example, the observant French visitor to America Alexis de Tocqueville offered a well-founded caution that balancing material self-interest with the needs of society would be a challenge the United States would face.

Yet these continental ideas were set loose across the wide-open plains of the uncharted Americas and evolved into the enshrined individual – a self of its own making – backed by a durable constitution safeguarding individual liberties. Thus the individual was now unfettered in its pursuit of private property ownership, self-recognition, and self-interest. And so, today, the Western outlook tends to go something like this: "I am independent and self-defined. I have personal rights and private property, and it is my right to protect them." In essence, "I am an island of my own making, and the main thing I need to rely on others and society for is to protect my rights and property."

However, our preference for individualism has led to the gradual dissolution of a shared identity and responsibility to community. Loneliness, isolation, and stunted emotional growth are real consequences that affect people of all ages and from all walks of life. The prevalence of both mental and physical illness have reached what experts and nonexperts agree are epidemic levels. For such a "developed" human society founded on the ideals of individualism, we seem to have a long list of crises to address.

In 1819, as the individual revolution continued in Western society, the U.S. Supreme Court made a landmark decision: to give the rights guaranteed to people (or more specifically at the time, white men) to the corporation.

The decision gave corporations a unique right to express their individualism and to act freely in their own interest to pursue profits and protect property on behalf of their owners. **Yet, crucially, despite receiving that right, corporations were not held to the same standard of responsibility or required to perform the moral duties expected of all other sorts of persons.**

Spurred on by the cultural preference for individualism and an underlying current of greed, corporations gradually exercised more and more freedom to act in their individual interests to the exclusion of the collective interest. **Wholesale exploitation of all sorts was justified as good business and performed under the premise of fiduciary duty because it was economically rational.** As corporations grew and the Industrial Revolution and technological advances transformed global relations and commerce, these corporations already trained to deliver profit with relentless precision gradually transformed into colossal global "selves," exploiting whatever they could to unearth new streams of profit. The application of corporate personhood we have grown used to is perhaps the ultimate expression of individualism: a paragon of selfishness with little concern for others.

As we gradually recalibrate our understanding of what it means to be a person and rebalance *ipse* with *idem,* self-reliance with communal bonds, and independence with responsibility to others, a predictable outcome is also occurring in business. That license for corporations to do anything so long as it turns a profit is being steadily revoked.

The individual revolution continues.

Rediscovering our selfless gene

Throughout human history, we have seen that to be truly human is to be a person for others. The greatest human distinction, it seems, is to relate to and serve other people. This tendency deserves a name. Let's call it *the selfless gene.*

In many ways, the problems we presently face are the result of generations of leadership (especially in business) that has, often unintentionally or by external decree, defied the selfless gene. Continuing to do so is now risky and even untenable, due to a rising tide of social pressure, and so in business we must quickly learn to embrace an entirely different set of priorities that recognize and support the selfless gene.

There are no culturally esteemed narratives celebrating the selfish egotists of society. Instead, our social commentaries warn us not to become them, for the misery and loneliness of Ebenezer Scrooge is usually the result. Culturally, we reject self-absorption almost without thinking, yet we accept and have even encouraged similar narcissism in business.

Many leaders are either aware of this reality or helping to state new priorities and chart new paths. However, many current leaders will be either unwilling or unequipped to do so. In the face of such vast and monumental change, if company leaders fail to recognize this selfless gene and do not learn to align their actions with it, the most likely outcomes are either a personal fall (think Jordan Belfort from *The Wolf of Wall Street*) or the collapse of the organization they lead (think Ken Lay and Enron).

A self-centered identity will generate selfishness and social inequality — we've learned that from experience. It is a change of identity that changes a culture, and social progress is always determined by moral progress, not economic or political forces. What would happen then, if we focused our unique selves and our businesses outward instead of inward, to serve others instead of ourselves?

Disquiet on the Western front

The West — and in particular the U.S. — is a giant social experiment that unfolded as a result of a fascinating concoction of social developments. As Western culture spread outward around the globe and Western society pressed on toward its maturity, opportunity emerged everywhere. In the past two centuries, more people have seized it than ever before. Innovation flourished, material quality of life soared, evil empires rose and were defeated, and the American Dream became a reality for many (not just Americans). Western society was proof that we could figure it out, and so we rode roughshod toward the millennium, more successful, it seemed, than ever.

The real truth is that we're not quite as perfect as we'd often like to think. The principles around which we have constructed Western society — namely rational self-interest and individualism — are less virtuous and humanistic than we had thought. The new era of human progress and prosperity we thought had arrived is actually fraught with grave danger, intractable problems, and refuse (both literal and figurative) from the path we took to get here. It is the failure of success. So many have begun to subconsciously wonder if the extreme preference we have given to rationalism and individualism over the past two centuries deserves a second look.

Despite the gains and improvements of "progress," an uncomfortable fact remains: There were consequences, and we are now experiencing them in full force. All is not well. The whole system we've built upon these key principles of rational self-interest and individualism has its share of ominous problems.

We are depleting our land and nonrenewable natural resources at a record pace. The natural environment we rely on suffers from pollution and degradation like never before and in ways that threaten our basic survival. The planet is getting warmer. According to the U.N. World Meteorological Organization, 15 of the 16 hottest years on record have occurred since 2000, and 2016 was the hottest on record, about 1 degree Celsius above the long term average. Stress on our planet is at its highest level in our history — mostly the result of human causes.

Aside from this, the Western experiment has also encumbered us with a number of social dysfunctions that are becoming more apparent. The rise in working- and single-parent families stresses community and family ties, and our levels of task-oriented busyness leave us at risk of social isolation. As these social dysfunctions grow, the workplace is not left unscathed. Gallup's research shows that "engagement among U.S. workers is holding steady at a scant 30%. This means seven out of ten people are either 'checked out,' or actively hostile toward their employers. Seven out of ten." This poll data suggesting 70% employee *dis*engagement is corroborated by the real-life experience of millions upon millions of people, many of whom long to work for better companies, where they can help tackle something that matters. As if those realities are not grim enough, we also see polarized, partisan political systems too feeble and hobbled to deal with the major issues of our time. All of this is set in the context of an aging population that has unearthed new social stresses, costs, and realities, not to mention a rapid and unprecedented urban migration that now locates more than 50% of the global population in cities (a 20% spike over a 60-year period).

Economically, things do not appear much better. The way we have utilized the tool of commerce has produced startling (and rising) income inequality and wealth disparity that threatens the fabled middle class.

New patterns of corporate instability have cropped up, not to mention the failure of massive publicly held companies deemed "too big to fail" and thus propped up by government bailouts. Internationally, entire countries in the intertwined web of global finance and government face default, inflation, and instability. Economically, slow growth is the new reality, and presumed stability has given way to a boom/bust cycle that seems only destined to grow in scale and impact.

As the risks and damages of the embedded system become more apparent, people are responding dynamically and resolutely, as they always have, causing a shift. The societal pendulum is swinging back toward a more natural balance between individualism and community, rationalism and belief. To be sure, such turbulence has happened before. The fundamental difference today is that those who feel this generations-old disquiet can find each other and swell into a chorus. The internet of ideas changes everything. And, as we are all aware, when a society chooses a new path, the shift in direction must also be reflected in business.

Commerce is an amoral institution, merely a tool at the disposal of the people who would use it. When its stewards fill it with a caustic solution of individualism and rationalism that disregards social imperatives and contravenes the natural law of *panarchy*, the damages caused are accelerated, and the unintended consequences are magnified. **The end product we have demanded of business — profit — is an impersonal figure devoid of human-relational meaning or any indication of social costs or recognition of the moral absolutes that hold society together.** Today, customers and employees are demanding that companies adjust their focus and the things they deliver (not to mention the way they deliver them) to account for unintended and externalized consequences.

Supercharged by social media and the internet, the demand for these fundamental shifts has become increasingly urgent.

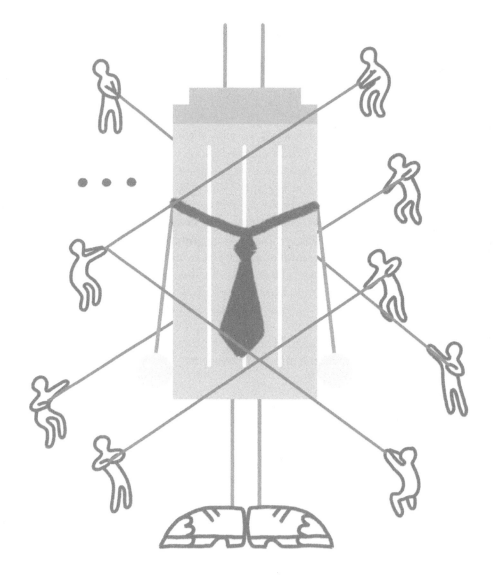

New demands of a fourth voice

When Chuck Prince's music stopped, throwing Citigroup and countless other corporate giants into disarray from which they may never fully recover, that circus tune did not give way to a silent void. Far from it. We have instead heard the babble of many once-muted voices – a gathering roar to be sure.

As businesses entered the 21st century, they were shaped by three powerful voices. The strongest (and still most powerful) voice driving public corporations is the voice of the market, mediated most visibly through quarterly reporting to analysts. This voice is supposed to channel shareholders who demand profitable, predictable growth. Hence, guidance is provided so expectations can be set and delivered, with management appearing to remain in control. This voice remains dominant, for to miss the numbers is still the cardinal sin of management in the belief system that guides public companies.

The second voice – the one that trails the first often by years or even decades – is the voice of the regulator. Largely a response to correct past deviance, regulations are a social mechanism of constraint for the willfully individualistic corporation. They are a costly burden to business (not to mention government) and a lagging, often reactionary system of constraints that are not designed to facilitate health, but rather to simply prevent abuse.

The third voice emerged in the late 20th century – Corporate Social Responsibility (CSR). As a battle cry, it has been a valid and well-intentioned attempt to inspire companies to do good while continuingto pursue their primary aim of extracting money from the marketplace.

It is a telling commentary on the state of affairs when compliance with a basic expectation of human behavior – social responsibility – is trotted out as a beacon of hope. It shows just how self-centered our business institutions have become. Without demeaning the importance of this change, for it is a good one, there is still something about celebrating CSR that feels like giving a trophy engraved "Left the Smallest Bruise" to the nicest of the playground bullies.

Although many who have led this CSR movement are bright, creative, diligent, and well-intentioned advocates, as a movement CSR has proved merely an addendum to the core corporate agenda.

An immensely powerful fourth voice has grown from a gentle hum in the background to a din louder than all other voices. It is the voice of the people – the everyday customer and employee – amplified by the digital disturbance of the internet and social media. The way we communicate and interact with one another and with companies has transformed.

Social media enables the mass fusing of individual experiences into a common, shared experience on an unprecedented scale. What was once a disconnected, agitated many has become a mobilized and very vocal unit. One negative experience is echoed by a host of other dissatisfied voices – people who feel the same way and can now join together for a common cause.

Today, no business of any scale can ignore its digital critics, and companies are learning to listen carefully. They are, in fact, the most influential voices to which it has ever had to pay attention. The global brand Goliaths, armed with all the power fostered by their substantive budgets, are no match for the million Davids who confront them armed with nothing but the slings of social media. The crux of this phenomenon is that the voice of customers and employees is becoming, perhaps once and for all, the most powerful voice of authority over business.

For instance, using social networks and an online petition tool called change. org, a Mississippi teenager named Sarah Kavanagh led a consumer revolt against PepsiCo. Thousands joined the action, the media was awakened, and a PR nightmare kicked into full gear. After only a few short weeks of this, PepsiCo was forced to remove from their recipes a popular North American soft drink additive called brominated vegetable oil (BVO), which had been shown to cause adverse health effects when consumed in large amounts. Rival The Coca-Cola Company scrambled to follow suit, and just like that, a huge industry was changed. Kavanagh told *USA Today,* "It's really good to know that companies, especially big companies, are listening to consumers." That's an understatement: A vocal teenager caused a major adjustment in a $100 billion market.

Naturally, prudent and adaptive businesses are heading in a welcome direction – toward honesty and transparency. Don Peppers and Martha Rogers suggest in their most recent work, *Extreme Trust,* that "if you want to succeed, you will need your customers to see you as reliable, dependable, credible, helpful, respectful, open, responsive, and honest. Whether you're any of these things or not, they'll still be telling their friends about you." Peppers and Rogers later conclude that trust is quickly becoming a basis of competitive advantage because "mere trustworthiness, fine until now, will no longer be enough to compete with companies that have figured out how to be genuinely trustable."

For those of us who wake up each morning thinking that it would be great if the world got a little better today rather than a little bit worse, this is a remarkably encouraging turn of events.

The fact that various publics can demand a positive shift and then exert enough pressure on corporate boards and executives to actually make it happen is not simply a trend; it's a new reality. In the future, successful business will be done not secretly but transparently and under the watchful eye of the public, who will be ready to exercise a more vocal governance and oversight than any board might have dared. We will be all the better for it.

The fourth voice is demanding more than just transparency. It is also requiring a new set of business priorities. While the market and regulators have sketched the field of play and CSR has helped focus the efforts of business, the new rules of the game are now being set: The CSR agenda is becoming *the* corporate agenda.

Millennials are making their demands known. They, unlike those before them, must stare down things like climate change and global poverty. Collectively, they have realized that they are the first generation that will need to solve major global problems just to live in a way that resembles the way they do now. Millennials are voicing new expectations of their employers and are setting new ground rules for the companies they're willing to buy from. For instance, a 2015 survey of millennials undertaken by Deloitte concluded that a sense of purpose is a major reason six in ten millennials work where they do. That same survey also found that only 58%

believe that businesses behave in an ethical manner. It went on to identify a number of significant gaps between what millennials would like the priorities, leadership, and positive impact of business to be and what they believe about its current state. For instance, the study concluded that "millennials would prioritize the sense of purpose around people rather than growth or profit maximization." Furthermore, the data from the 2011 edition of this same series of surveys indicated that 92% of millennials believe business success should be measured by more than profit.

These trends and opinions are consistent with the balance of research on the largest living generation and the largest generational segment of the U.S. workforce (as of Q1 2015). A large percentage of this generation entered that same workforce during The Great Recession and therefore faced high levels of underemployment or unemployment. As a whole, millennials have been convincingly identified as being "unmoored from institutions."

The fourth voice — this voice of customers and employees that booms with millennial undertones — says that business must deliver something greater than profit: solutions to real social problems.

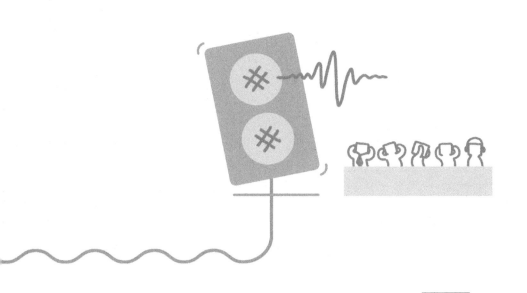

PURPOSE FOR BUSINESS:
A BYPRODUCT OF UNREST

Over the past decade or so, as customers and employees have made noise about business solving social problems, this rising din has reached the ears of forward-thinking and prudent marketers and business minds, many of whom have responded as they have been taught: shift the offering, tweak the language, and pivot toward the space of business opportunity.

The business response is materializing, and the dynamic between both business and society is changing. For instance, at a recent World Business Forum in New York, the entire first day of the conference was filled with references to the social impacts of business without a single reference to economic performance. I was there, and I listened carefully.

But, a word to the wise: there are many effective marketing tools. Purpose is not one of them. Any "purpose-washing" will leave a mark.

Wander through a bookstore or a glance at some of the notable business journals and you'll find evidence that a business response to an entirely new set of demands has begun. Every day, more and more is written that expresses a growing dissatisfaction with the way business interacts with society. Much of that literature also envisions new ways of running a business that begin to reverse the damage wrought. In just the past few years, we've seen titles like *Start with Why, The Human Brand,* and *Firms of Endearment* among many others.

In boardrooms, around water coolers, and from podiums across business, points of view are being lauded that 15 years ago would have been met with silence or even incredulous laughter. They are phrases like:

- "People don't buy what you do, they buy why you do it."

- "Authenticity is the new coin of the realm."

- "… in a more socially connected, transparent world – a world of Twitter and Facebook, WikiLeaks and YouTube – companies will be held accountable by customers for proactively protecting their interests, rather than simply passively refraining from cheating them or deceiving them."

- "… we are loyal to the people behind companies and brands, not their products, prices, or loyalty programs."

Clearly, businesspeople sense the disillusionment of a restless public. They are responding with a noble, well-intentioned effort that boasts an increasingly sound business case: to bend their businesses toward some form of social purpose.

There are already numerous experimentations that involve incorporating various tweaks, rebalances, and new dimensions to business as usual. They are things such as the balanced scorecard, the triple bottom line, shared value, and even benefit corporations, a relatively new designation which legally protects social mission as a valid corporate intention. All are worthy attempts to anticipate and implement an emerging but still very unstable new model for business. Companies are springing up in this new space or migrating toward it, proving along the way that business success and enduring value for society can coincide. Many of these new expressions are built on creative, inventive business models that turn convention on its ear.

Business Model Type	Example
Buy One, Give One	TOMS, Warby Parker
Social Impact Investing	Community/Social Impact Bonds, Responsible Investment (RI), Global Impact Investing Network (GIIN)
Community-Shared	Co-ops, community solar projects, community-supported agriculture projects (CSAs)
Peer-to-Peer	Airbnb, Etsy, Uber

As this business response continues to materialize, new reporting methods, certifications, and recognitions that promote good business and responsible corporate behavior turn up regularly.

Reporting Method	Description
Environmental Profit & Loss Statement (EP&L)	Designed to convert environmental effects of business activities into financial metrics
International Integrated Reporting <IR> Framework	Focused on value creation and the capitals used by the business to create value over time
Impact Reporting and Investment Standards (IRIS) metrics	Designed to measure the social, environmental, and financial performance of an investment

Certification	Description
B Corp Certification	Standards for verified social and environmental performance, public transparency, and legal accountability and confirmation of intent to use the power of markets to solve social and environmental problems
Leadership in Energy and Environmental Design (LEED) Certification	Benchmarks for design, construction, and operation of green buildings
Green Business Bureau	Engages key stakeholders to determine sustainability certification and initiatives

Recognition	Description
The Civic 50	Honors the 50 most community-minded companies in the U.S.
Fortune "Change the World" List	Partnership between *Fortune,* Shared Value Institute, and the social change consultancy FSG to evaluate large companies ($1bn + revenue) for impact, business results, and innovation
The Global 100	Index of the most sustainable corporations in the world

It's fascinating to see a change in methods and innovation unfold around how a business delivers its value, who receives that value, and how that value is measured.

Lurking behind these legitimate and well-intentioned efforts to scratch the "purpose for business" itch in an age of authenticity and high demand for corporate transparency is a lethal risk: reality.

What real outcomes are resulting from this abundance of interest in the subject of purpose? In 2015, *Harvard Business Review* and Ernst & Young put forward a report entitled *The Business Case for Purpose*. The writers of the study discovered that while 89% of the business leaders whom they interviewed suggested that purpose matters, only 37% said that the business model and operations of the organization were well aligned with its purpose. Purpose in theory is solid. Purpose in reality is sorely lacking.

This suggests that despite declarations, wishes, and best intentions, profit still ranks as the most important aim businesses are pursuing, and management and ownership either lack the will to change that or haven't yet figured out how. This is not surprising, nor should it be guilt-inducing – it is simply the reality. Old habits die hard, especially in stressful times, and rooting them out will require constant vigilance. This reality demands the utmost care in the way leaders deal with their company's purpose, for the lure of fakery and the inability to deliver on purpose will prove disastrous in the age of authenticity and such high demand for corporate transparency.

We don't need a business case for purpose, what we need is a purpose case for business.

Purpose-washing will leave a mark

"Purpose, schmurpose," muttered the seasoned PR executive as we reviewed an early draft in the development of this very book. "Purpose is everywhere these days, and so much of it has the feeling of being just the newest form of marketing campaignery in one way or another."

I saw unmistakable signs of this on a trip to New York. The ads on the inflight entertainment have huckstered financial investments under the purpose umbrella for a while, but when I caught sight of the promotions for Justin Bieber's *Purpose* tour in the back of my taxi, I knew the word needed to be reclaimed. I was instantly glad to have some years ago selected an old Greek word (more on that later) referencing "intended end" as the backbone of my writing on this subject of purpose in business, for it will undoubtedly bring helpful clarity as we make some sense of all of this cacophony around purpose.

My friend in PR is right. "Purpose, schmurpose." It so often feels like just another fad, another concert tour, another purpose-branding tagline, another campaign – all evidence of a new agenda of purpose-washing. When the real intent is to do well, a purpose can be cynically conceived and superficially applied, then discarded when it inevitably proves too challenging or costly to the real agenda. But disingenuous companies simply will not be abided, and when the purpose frauds are discovered – and there are plenty – they will end up much farther down the road to ruin than if they had honestly declared their intentions, no matter how selfish or shortsighted. In other cases, like new wine into old wineskins, some corporate systems may not be pliable enough to handle the new life and complexity that a purpose beyond profit implies, despite earnest wishes to live up to it. The truth is that if a company declares a purpose, it must be accountable to it.

There are many effective marketing tools. Purpose is not one of them.

The fourth voice has little tolerance for inauthenticity. Using a socially conscious purpose simply because it may produce marketing or economic gain is a dangerous game. Not only does it spring from the fleeting (but familiar) logic that profit is king, it completely misses the fundamental rethink that is underway. Society is not asking for the business case for purpose. What society is in fact demanding to see is the purpose case for business. We must not confuse the two.

It is much easier to point out and try to fix what is broken in an old model than to predict and courageously choose an entirely new and better way. Now that we've done the former, let's explore what the latter might look like.

"*Purpose*"

FOR GOODNESS' SAKE:
BUSINESS FOR TELOS

We are in the midst of an era of significant social change coinciding with growing economic uncertainty due to our fascination with single-variable optimization of profit that has contradicted the natural rule of panarchy. Turbulence is difficult, but it also creates the ideal conditions for impactful change. We have before us a unique opportunity to fundamentally alter the way business works.

We can alter the very purpose of business from merely delivering profit to delivering something far more meaningful — positive social impact. This will feel like a radical idea, given our existing notion of business. But it is far more sensible that business should benefit society rather than benefit only itself and its owners at society's expense — which is so often the case.

If our companies are going to survive and thrive in the turbulence of a now unstable system, we must determine and adopt a more thoughtful, balanced way to manage and rehabilitate the systems we rely on — economic ones included. Doing so will require clear thinking and courageous leadership. It will require the hard work of choosing to adhere to a new business mandate from society, and it will bring the discomfort of facing a new and unplanned future. Such change is underway, one heart and mind at a time.

We are in the midst of a fundamental reconsideration of the very priorities of business and the reasons we engage in economic activities. The way the structures we create around those economic activities interact with society is in the midst of transformation. What results from this transformation is yet to be determined. However, it is quickly becoming reality that business rotates on a new moral axis and functions *for goodness' sake*. This is not by any means a utopia, but it is demonstrably better than what we have experienced so far.

We cannot afford, as a human race, to waste the opportunity presented. The common applications of purpose for business and doing good for the sake of doing well simply do not cause a large enough angle of trajectory for the vector of change. We need a new aim for business — not just a marketing rethink for the way companies talk about themselves in order to keep serving their financial bottom line.

The fact of the matter is this: As long as we treat purpose as a management technique that can be harnessed to achieve an old set of ends — shareholder value maximization by any (even noble) means — we will miss the point completely. This is not about a valid business case for purpose that can just be more effectively implemented. We must face the stark reality that our current social and environmental conditions actually present a purpose case for the existence of business.

We do not need purposes that further existing business interests. We need businesses that relentlessly deliver on a telos to serve others.

Telos

A Greek word meaning "intended end." Applied by Aristotle to humans, telos implies a life of virtue, lived for the good of others. Telos has an inherent benevolence and a predisposition toward the common good. It is most precisely defined as a purpose-for-others. Every telos is a purpose, but only the rare purpose is a telos.

My colleague Angela described this quite succinctly after an aha moment. She called me the other day to say that her whole way of thinking had been turned upside down. Long a subscriber to the fairly new shared value model promulgated by Harvard's Michael Porter, Angela believed that companies could indeed, as she put it, do well by doing good. But as she sat and listened to a group of executives from a very well-known global brand lay out their social mission without any reference to its business case, she began to see something different.

Curious, Angela persistently questioned these leaders with the expectation that she would eventually uncover the economic rationalization for their decision to invest significantly in making a major social contribution. What she came to discover was that their decision had nothing to do with economic factors — they were just doing what they were convinced was right for the world.

"In shared value, we think we can do well by doing good, but I now realize that we have to do good and we just *might,* if we are lucky and smart, do well," she explained later. The decision those business leaders made to do what they thought was right for the world produced all manner of positive economic outcomes in the end. By choosing good first, the decisions made by those business leaders resonated with both customers and employees alike, especially the latter, such that the business case (which never was one) ended up a slam dunk. This is what the radical idea of selecting a telos simply because it is meaningful and not for its impact on the bottom line can look like. But that is not always the case. The hard truth is that we will have to become satisfied with the reality that financial success may not come and that simply doing the right thing (and helping another person) is positive outcome enough. That is a major bridge to cross, given where we are today.

For that reason, the adoption of a telos by a business involves the reformulation or clarification of the very identity of the organization and its primary reason to exist. This is no fad. Leaders cannot simply adopt purpose as yet another management technique that they can use to bend an organization to their will. Rather, they will find that the telos they subscribe to actually directs them in accordance with a drive much larger than their own intentions. They will find themselves less in control of an agenda and more compelled by a course, even a calling.

For instance, the 2015 Paris Agreement, which limits climate change to 1.5 degrees Celsius, is binding and has been signed by 195 countries. The necessary targets set out will not, of course, be reached without businesses that decide to pursue related goals because it is simply the right thing to do. At a fundamental level, organizational change must be preceded by personal change. Only when you and I and our peers change will real and lasting transformation occur in our organizations.

If that seems daunting, it is. But take heart, others have gone before.

Others have gone before

From 1973 to 1994, Ray Anderson founded a carpet manufacturing company and led its explosive growth into the leading global manufacturer of modular carpet tiles for residential and commercial use. Ray and his colleagues at Interface spent years perfecting an industrial-scale, resource-intensive, linear method of production and distribution. Profits were high. Growth was rapid, and prospects were good. By all the old measures of business success, they were knocking it out of the park. Ray Anderson should have sold his company for a pile of cash and left the game. '

Except Ray Anderson wasn't going to leave that way. Triggered by his own deeply personal change of heart and mind, Anderson was moved by the conviction that as the head of a resource-intensive manufacturing business, he was a plunderer of the earth.

His own words describe this radical turning point best:

> I once told a *Fortune Magazine* writer that someday people like me would go to jail. And that became the headline of a *Fortune* article ... theft is a crime. And theft of our children's future would someday be a crime. But I realized, for that to be true — for theft of our children's future to be a crime — there must be a clear, demonstrable alternative to the take-make-waste industrial system that so dominates our civilization.⁵

Ray Anderson knew that business and industry were wrecking the planet, but in a piercing bit of irony, he also understood that business was the institution most likely to be able to reverse previous wrongs and lead us out of the mess we made. He determined to start doing something about it personally. "If not us, then who?" he thought, echoing some of the most fundamental Western ethics. He issued a challenge to his company to "do no harm," and to that, he added "take nothing from the environment."

Today, many are doing their part by reshaping the companies we've got and by conceiving new businesses according to a blueprint other than the one we've always known. They are leaders like Neil, David, Jeffrey, and Andrew, who founded Warby Parker. They are people like my friend Tim, who has pushed his company to become a certified B Corp because he thought it was the right thing to do. They are people who sit around the corner from you or work in your office building or who might occasionally visit the coffee shop down the street. But make no mistake; one by one, they are creating a new future for business.

In that future, businesses will exist to solve important social problems and meet important social needs at every strata and on every scale from global to very local. Work and its corollary, employment – that human endeavor essential for mental and physical health – will feel meaningful and be worthwhile. The realities of *panarchy* will spur the creation and growth of resilient companies that deliver across a wide swath of variables, profit included. Profit will remain an important part of business activity because it is a vital means of attracting sufficient capital and will allow the company to deliver its purpose with greater scale and impact for the long term. But profit will no longer be a sole – or even primary – aim. It will recede into a slot next to other vital organizational factors we measure and pay close attention to, like employee engagement, sales, and customer retention. The possession of greater resources (in other words, being a large company) will be desirable not because it somehow guarantees competitive advantage but because it allows for greater scale and quality of positive social impact and can provide for better delivery of that which the public demands.

Finally, and most important, business – and its largest component part, the corporation – will be less the instrument of traders whose goal is to extract monetary gains and more the instrument and recipient of careful stewardship by owners whose personal commitment to the corporation's telos is evident.

Nature and the complex systems of the world – the economy included – are resilient. A long list of positive developments suggests that in both business and in life, this shift demanded by the fourth voice has been building for some years – generations in fact. Broken systems are rebounding, depleted ecosystems are being cared for and even restored, and in business, new kinds of companies are flourishing, while the dysfunctional dinosaurs are dying. Previously unfathomable business models are not just the stuff of dreams, they are real and thriving. Innovation is on the rise, and people are doing lots of good for one another.

As is often the case in the midst of a monumental and historic pivot, there is a choice, and it is a consequential one: Will we aid the shift from profit as purpose to profit that serves purpose, or will we stand in its way? It is a real choice that each of us must make each day.

Many people are already choosing this change for the better. However, to spur the shift will still prove immensely challenging, especially at first. The ones who are standing up to lead the charge are hopeful realists – people with a rare mix of perspective and creativity, wits and wisdom, enthusiasm and restraint, courage and character. They understand the strength of some of the forces driving this change and sense the growing swell of hope. But most importantly, they have an insatiable desire to uncover the most important value a company can ever create: the delivery of social good. Quite simply, they have chosen the other over themselves. This is what it means to be uniquely human, to be personal, to be for the other. It is a characteristic that businesses we'll call *purposeful enterprises* choose.

A new kind of company: The purposeful enterprise

Many of you are gradually creating a new future for business and a new kind of company, one built for goodness' sake: the purposeful enterprise.

Purposeful enterprise

A company that continually strives to live out its telos, a pursuit which encodes the telos into the identity of the organization as both culture (where the telos can be clearly and truthfully lived out) and brand (where the telos can be clearly and truthfully expressed externally).

The path to become a purposeful enterprise will be a difficult one, perhaps even nearly impossible, but such odds didn't stop the quality movement of the 1970s and 80s from making known its goal of zero defects. That aspiration remains unfulfilled, yet in the process of striving toward that distant objective with hope, the manufacturing industry has been revolutionized and vastly improved.

Those with the courage and determination to discover the *telos* of their organization and pursue it may one day realize that aspiration. But even if they don't, they will undoubtedly have pushed their companies to be better than they are today. This intentional movement toward *telos* is something we'll call *telosity.*

Telosity

A word we'll use to convey the accelerating movement of a business toward a telos. With the usage of the suffix *-ity*, meaning state or quality, the word *telosity* describes being in a state of telos, which necessitates constant movement toward the fulfillment of that telos. The pronunciation of the word, like *velocity*, is intentional and another reference to the movement in a specific direction that telos implies.

Complex systems like businesses, not to mention our whole system of commerce, have huge momentum, and the way they change direction is either by gradual realignment one degree at a time, or by coming perilously close to tumbling off a cliff, which forces significant realignment and effort to gain momentum on an entirely new path. In other words, good things tend to happen slowly, while failure is rapid and usually disastrous. According to the *panarchy* cycle — in which optimizing a single variable will eventually destabilize the whole system, introducing an unpredictable entropy — reorganization (the gradual realignment) is bound to follow the collapse.

But if we act now and act courageously, we may yet be able to skirt the collapse altogether by choosing a different path and cultivating system resilience.

THE CHARACTER OF EVERY
PURPOSEFUL ENTERPRISE

There are three core elements that compose the identity of every organization: brand, culture and purpose.

The outward expression of an organization's identity (brand) and the inward manifestation of that identity (culture) are well known, but the third element, one that is less visible yet deeply significant, is purpose.

Every organization has a purpose, whether it is clearly articulated or not. Some organizations (purposeful enterprises, to be specific) have a purpose-for-others — what we call a telos.

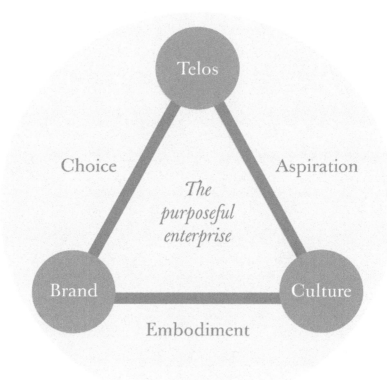

The system of three interrelated elements (telos, brand and culture) that comprise the organizational identity of every purposeful enterprise and the three levers (aspiration, choice and embodiment) that help us influence them (covered in the next section).

When the following are true, a purposeful enterprise comes to life:

- The organization is held together by the pursuit of a *telos* that answers the question "Who are we in service to others?" in a way that is meaningful to its stakeholders, reflects the organization's identity, and serves as a guiding star to inform all decisions.

- The organization's brand fully, seamlessly, and authentically declares the *telos* so that the outward-facing identity of the company leads the way and connects with the world as an expression of both a social license and a well-understood, internally defined identity that is formed by choices that reflect the *telos*.

- The organization is propelled forward in its culture by the aspiration employees have for the *telos* and animated by the actions they each take every day in support of it through the system of relationships, norms, and structures that comprise the company culture.

- Reflecting one another as they are embodied by the organization, brand and culture align so that what the company claims about itself (brand, external identity) is the same as what is seen every day in the life of the company (culture, internal identity), triggering organizational movement in the direction of the *telos* — telosity.

When brand and culture truly serve the *telos*, it holds the organization together and moves it forward. And it builds trust with employees and consumers (who are, effectively, the same people), such that they might ultimately say things like "That company has a lot of integrity."

The purposeful enterprise represents our best attempt to capture this emerging movement that is beginning to deliver the kind of system change and social benefits that society requires.

Telos: An organization's purpose-for-others

Every purposeful enterprise is built around a *telos* to put its best work into creating social value. It serves others outside the enterprise. It must be repeated: Profit is not a *telos* in the sense of the word as we have defined it. Neither is making the best and most recommended widget. Those are goals or intentions, but they are not compelling enough reasons for being. As Daniel Pink identifies in his book *Drive,* "Humans, by their nature, seek purpose … a cause greater and more enduring than themselves." In other words, a purpose-for-others. A *telos*.

To help your organization discover its *telos*, you must find a thoughtful answer to the fundamental question "Who are we in service to others?" Locating this answer will take time and significant organizational reflection, but it may help to know that a *telos* has four duties.

A *telos* must:

> Satisfy the selfless gene. **Deep down, we all have a desire to do good for others. A *telos* scratches that almighty itch by delivering a social good outside the company. Important caveat: Serving owners and shareholders with profit growth or market penetration does not satisfy the selfless gene.**

> Prove true as it is embodied. **Good intentions are not enough. If they are not lived out, they are a manipulation, even a mask. A *telos* is true, and therefore trusted, because it is made alive by real people.**

> Deliver meaning **by striving for an innovative solution to a worthy problem. A *telos* is a big, "leave the world a better place" goal that offers significance to those who work toward it. Important caveat: Merely creating economic value will not stand up as a worthy enough goal to deliver significance, especially for millennials.**

> Unite people and transform them **into something greater than the sum of their parts. A *telos* is a uniting force that is both personal and communal.**

Brand integrity that declares the telos

Beyond the core identity built around the pursuit of a *telos*, purposeful enterprises are defined and set apart by their brands, which must be authentic and declare the *telos*.

Both consumers and employees increasingly demand transparency and authenticity. There is a danger here. Authenticity can be delivered with the same selfish narcissism and rampant individualism that are part of the problem with today's culture.

If authenticity alone is not enough, what else does a purposeful enterprise need? The quality of *integrity* is the answer, and it is something that must be earned. The purposeful enterprise is not merely an organization that declares its reason for being in an authentic manner. Rather, its customers, employees, suppliers, and others experience this authentic expression of brand and testify to the integrity of the organization. There is congruence between the words they hear and the actions they observe. Authenticity can be claimed, but integrity can only be conferred.

Similarly, in a world where brand identities are becoming bestowed as much as earned, all companies must now be granted a social license to operate. The EBCs of Branding show the way:

The Exemplar Test – Analog or digital media may help communicate a concept, but outbound media matters less and less. A brand has credibility when it is activated by employees. In other words, a brand is activated by employee engagement inasmuch as exemplars in the organization make a brand idea tangible and accessible to those who hear it.

The Blooper Test – All companies are bound to make mistakes or come under fire for something. The way a company handles these bloopers will show the true colors of the brand (and the people who represent it).

The Connection Test – This one is simple. How much do people care about and connect with the brand and the ideals it stands for? What kind of emotional resonance and connection does the brand create? The best evidence of a strong connection is when people get so excited about a brand that they can't help but tell all their friends.

An animating culture that proves the telos

Beyond the pursuit of *telos* and the evidence of brand integrity, the third element that sets the purposeful enterprise apart is its culture, which must animate the brand and prove the *telos*. Such a culture is marked by three essential habits: aligned aspirations, consistent choice, and embodiment.

The first of these habits, aligned aspirations, is always evident in early-stage businesses where many of the founding members are there because they share the passion to build something together. Even in more mature, often larger organizations, there can still exist the potential for common hopes and desires. One such organization that I know well comprises a critical mass of associates who delight in making unexpected good things happen for consumers.

Second, the culture of a purposeful enterprise is marked by the kinds of choices that are made, often by senior management, that comprise what is usually referred to as *strategy*. It is also animated by the choices of message that are made. In every organization, there is an abundance of opportunity to say something through consistent choices, even if that means being silent. The reluctance of one organization to speak about a recent failure in a product launch is a powerful signal that shapes the culture, while in another, their Dare to Try Award symbolizes the intention to embrace risks, regardless of success.

Third, and perhaps most powerful, the culture of the purposeful enterprise is shaped profoundly by the principles embodied by its heroes and leaders. The embodiment of a *telos* by a handful of influencers (who may simply be those who decide to take a stand for the *telos*, regardless of their status in the organization) inevitably lifts the standards of behavior for all to new heights and leads others toward a better way. These exemplary leaders seek out passion for the *telos* in others. They mentor and nurture it, helping to bring to life the same energy and enthusiasm that they find they are unable to suppress in themselves. These are the evangelists – those whose enthusiasm is simply irrepressible – and their passion is infectious.

The familiar phrase "the apple does not fall far from the tree" applies not only to parenting but to influential leadership. Enthusiasm and belief in something worthwhile are passed on, and they resonate. I vividly remember two speeches by two leaders in the same organization where I was once employed. One dulled my emerging convictions, while the other stirred them. Soon, there was a transition, and the inspiring leader left the organization. I was not far behind, because I could feel conviction vanishing within myself and the organization under the direction of the uninspiring leader.

If, in your organization, you begin to feel the habitual alignment of aspirations and growing consistency of choice, and you recognize more leaders embodying something like a *telos* but you still wonder how the culture is coming along, there is one most revealing indicator to look for.

The standards of behavior may be rising by the day, and a more telling embodiment of the *telos* visible in each area of the business, but better performance according to *telos* is not enough. A significant reorganization of the framework and metrics the organization uses to measure performance must occur. A *telos* may be claimed and written on the wall, but until it is an integral part of the performance management system, it cannot really come to life. An organization with a *telos* statement to "make workplaces safe for every person" will disconnect its actions from that goal and demotivate its people if it measures and rewards success based only on revenue targets!

This brings us to elephant in the room: Becoming a purposeful enterprise will involve a massive change initiative that will go far beyond the simple attitudes and tactics we've explored.

Transforming an existing profit-centric organization into a purposeful enterprise may require years of attention and work and will likely involve transformation across every facet of the organization. And yet, despite usual limitations on such a change like budget, process, time, and the immense impatience of our age, there is no more dynamic motivator than *telos*, which can speed the pace of change and spur rapid transformation across the organization. We'll devote the remainder of our time to exploring some practical ways you can bring a purposeful enterprise to life.

HOW TO BRING A PURPOSEFUL ENTERPRISE TO LIFE

Across the field from my log-house office on the farm where I live, there is a grove of sugar maples that yield their precious sweetness to us each spring. A few years ago, these woods were marred by a vicious ice storm, the scars from which still disfigure the canopy and the ground below.

Already, new saplings are rushing up toward the holes of daylight left by felled giants, and as I walk through these woods, I am often struck by how fast the forest floor is changing. New growth races toward the light, blocking the old pathways and rearranging once-familiar scenery. It is good — abundant new life — but it is also change, and I look to the old trees that I will still rely on for syrup-making and wonder how long they will continue to stand. It is tempting to cut many of them down, harvest their timber, and attempt to speed the new crop of trees to replace them.

We face the same realities in business.

A forest ecosystem is an apt metaphor for where we are in business today. With the winds of change tearing through the canopy at gale force, and this migration toward *telos* exerting huge pressure on the biggest hardwoods, it is tempting to simply wait for them to fall and then redistribute their assets so there is room for a new generation of companies. After all, it is much easier to plant a purposeful enterprise from scratch, as a growing number of young entrepreneurs are doing today, than to prune and retrain an older organization to fit the new mold.

And yet, every established business is fully capable of the kind of change that is required to become a purposeful enterprise, and we will need scores of these old-growth hardwoods that enrich the landscape of business to do just that. Regrowth and arboreal maturity do not occur quickly in the maple forest. Neither will such regrowth happen quickly in business should many of the familiar giants suffer the same fate as those majestic maples in the ice storm. We will all be better off if the strength of these old-growth businesses can be redirected and fundamental change enacted so that they can function and flourish as purposeful enterprises for many years to come.

Organization systems theory suggests that while fundamental change is aided by the simpler levers for change like new structures, procedures, or practices, any lasting change is a result of movement in three critical domains – what Burke and Litwin have called "transformational variables." They are strategy, culture, and leadership.

Through these variables, we will be able to reshape the organizations where we serve. However, we need to overcome at least one barrier before we begin. We need to reconceive these three variables, because they have become hackneyed and overused. A business organization will begin to live out a *telos* when its people focus on the transformational levers of *choice* (of which strategy is an element), *aspiration* (which drives healthy culture), and most significant of all, *embodiment* (the most critical mark of leadership). We'll look now at how those are brought to life.

Transformational lever #1 — Choice

Businesses, both good and bad, do not emerge from articles or books like this one. They emerge from the accumulated daily choices of many, many people. Similarly, their essential character is not changed by administrative fiat or executive decree. In an interview, the former CEO of a major car company was asked what it was like to wield such power. He replied, "I am like a fly on a log, hurtling down a water chute with a 90-degree turn at the bottom, and all I can do is waggle my leg in the water and yell at the top of my voice, 'Whoa, you son of a bitch, whoa!'" We tend to assume that senior officers have far more influence over the business system than they do.

The enterprise that becomes purposeful does not do so solely because of extraordinary leadership, though that helps. Instead, it is a host of small yet intentional decisions — made by extraordinary leaders, yes, but also by every rank-and-file member of the organization — that accumulate to produce a cascade of movement in a positive direction. For instance, the CEO who chooses not to hold distracting quarterly calls with financial analysts has exercised leadership to do something impactful, but more important, she has managed to recognize and make a choice that many of her peers thought did not exist.

Personal choices lie at the heart of change. A choice made by the consumer to buy sustainably harvested fish or to pay slightly more for organic produce; a choice made by the buyer who changes suppliers over illegal working conditions or by the subordinate who brings the ethics violation to the boss's attention; a choice made by the new recruit who values meaning over position or by the investor who values social responsibility over maximized short-term financial return.

In the purposeful enterprise, employees challenge actions when they are inconsistent with the brand promise. Empty claims are called out by data, difficult budget decisions are challenged by the *telos*, and headcount allocations are judged against what it really takes to deliver the brand promise. Some individuals who perform exceptionally well in some domains but not in accordance with core values will be passed over for promotion or even dismissed. Executive compensation will be tied to long-term support of the *telos*, communications won't promise what can't be delivered, and board members will challenge the pragmatism of short-term benefits. These standards, actions, and behaviors are choices — a whole set of forks in the road that must be navigated with consistency to the *telos*.

Such choices can inspire people inside and outside the business. In fact, this is a desired outcome of all good strategy: to push people to opt in and do their part.

Often, these moments are triggered because when the *telos* is activated through strategy, extraneous parts of the business appear on the chopping block. It is where branding, marketing, and communications get their start. It is where goals and targets are set. It is where market strategies and product sequences are defined and supply chains, cost structures, and pricing are determined. And it is the first chance business leaders have to make choices that align with the *telos*.

The strategy choices that are made have great significance, not just because they set future plans and direction for the organization but also because of the simple fact that people are watching. Choices matter, and painful ones speak volumes to all who are aware of them.

To a remarkable degree, businesses — especially large ones — move because of a profound inertia. Many years ago, my colleague Mike Davidson and I fashioned a simple analysis of what happened when one generation of management inherited a large market share from the previous generation. Such an occurrence nurtured the misguided belief among the new generation that the solid performance of the business and the rewards they enjoyed derived from their own decisions and actions, when in fact, they were a legacy bestowed by a previous generation of wisdom. We called it "the poisoned inheritance."

In the purposeful enterprise, intention rules the day — not inertia. Each purposeful enterprise will carefully and intentionally locate its *telos*, its answer to the question "Who are we in service to others?" And once it has found that *telos*, it will have found something that both creates relevance and compels action. Products and services reflect the true purpose of the business and not mere market opportunism, and the brand creates and expresses an identity that reflects the *telos* in action. There are no intentional mixed messages.

Transformational lever #2 — Aspiration

Now, we exit the logical domain of strategy and choice and land squarely in the soft stuff of aspiration. Over the past 10 to 15 years, what was once soft stuff has become a lot harder. It now plays a central role in business thinking, planning, and execution alongside financial statements and capital budgets. Most thoughtful leaders have long known that it is the human side of the enterprise that is much harder, but more worthwhile, to engage than the mechanical and financial assets. And, as if to prove that point, John P. Kotter's article "Leading Change: Why Transformation Efforts Fail" suggests that it's usually the soft stuff that causes business change to fail.
So we turn to the issues of organizational culture.

Perhaps even the mention of the word *culture* in a business context brings to mind the classic remark usually attributed to famed author, consultant, and father of modern management Peter Drucker: "Culture eats strategy for breakfast." He was right. Once the choice has been made to initiate any sort of change process, culture is the first territory that must be crossed. But what is culture?

Some years ago, Ed Schein, a thought leader in organizational development theory, composed perhaps the clearest definition of this soft area of business. Schein defined culture as "the shared, taken-for-granted, implicit assumptions that a group holds and that determine how it perceives, thinks about, and reacts to its various environments." It's accurate and helpful, but it still feels rather remote and academic.

Corporate cultures do not spring from words, hopes, or even powerful ideas. Like strategy, culture arises from and is made real by the actions and decisions of real people. Therefore, the relentless habits of people — and over time, the little decisions about what does and does not matter — are what sustain or erode a culture.

A healthy culture must be actively stewarded — tied to a legacy of deliberate, consistent, and courageous habitual actions. The best place to look for a clear view of culture is how we interact when the boss isn't looking. That is often where the culture exists unencumbered, to be observed in its most natural form.

All of this comes with a very important qualifier: The culture of an organization is a human, animated reality that exists only to the extent that it is embodied. To dissect and rationalize an organization's culture as if it were an inanimate object is to deny its depth and uniqueness — and humanity. A healthy culture cannot fruitfully emerge until business leaders can discover and tap into their employees' aspirations to do something meaningful through their work.

Transformational lever #3 — Embodiment

Leadership is a hackneyed term. Too often, it only means a title and position of (sometimes iffy) responsibility — when it should refer to a person's ability to build trust, to influence, and to bring others along to places they did not believe they could reach. Chances are you know someone with these gifts. Now imagine if your organization began to fill up with them. That thought is why we're after this kind of leadership — a leadership of *gravitas,* cultivated by quality of character and the ability to connect with others to bring out the best in them.

Our preoccupation with outcomes leads us to focus our leadership behavior on technique and method. We argue pragmatically, "If I engage certain behavior, I will get certain results." Mountains of leadership literature trumpet methods, techniques, and formulae founded on the search for what works, emphasizing outcomes over people and ends over means. The professionalizing of our roles leads us to transact more and relate less, to be busier than we are reflective, to do more and be less. We have tended to turn the role of a leader into a desired collection of behaviors without requiring a more fundamental grounding in the foundations of identity.

As Rob Goffee and Gareth Jones explain in *Why Should Anyone Be Led by You?,* most leadership literature we see today comes from a strong psychological bias because it focuses on characteristics that leaders can display or the techniques they can employ. "The underlying assumption is that leadership is something we do to other people. But in our view, leadership should be seen as something we do with other people. Leadership must always be viewed as a relationship between the leader and the led." I prefer to go even further and suggest that leadership is who we are when we deal with others. It is an expression of identity rather than a portfolio of skills. To lead is not to think or to manipulate for good performance, but rather to be. Hence, we will use the term *embodiment* to make all the more evident that the leader is not one whose actions get certain results but whose actions reflect innate characteristics and virtues and an orientation of
being for the sake of the other.

Culture change happens person to person, and regardless of role or place in the organization, the way each person acts, manages, and leads has the potential to instigate others to take up the telos as their own. Indeed, every organization comprises individuals who are already taking action toward some purpose. The question is: What purpose?

The main source of such instigation is the leader's embodiment of the very *telos* she desires her followers to take up. If her organization has gotten its *telos* right, her followers' shared aspirations will begin to become real when she embodies it. New habits and behaviors are far more likely to be adopted when real people embody them.

Embodiment breaks down behavioral barriers that have been set by existing actions, culture, or predecessors, freeing courageous and noticeable actions to lift the everyday standard of behavior to new heights. Bringing *telos* to life will necessarily require you to cross some well-established boundaries. You will be able to identify the sort of behaviors necessary to embody the *telos* because in them, you will see courage and tolerance for discomfort.

At one level, this lever for change seems so simplistic, almost facile. To write about it seems to merely state the obvious. And yet typically, this sort of how-to literature is so enamored with method, technique, and the art of manipulation in all its many forms, that to advocate for a simple embrace of a purpose – indeed a *telos* – through embodiment, not as a means to an end, but because it is innately worthwhile, is almost revolutionary.

Over the past few years, as I have sought to articulate this emerging form of business that we call the purposeful enterprise, most of the friends and colleagues who have engaged my thinking on these matters have asked me to address the *how* of organizational change: "How do we transform our existing businesses?" It is a valid but vexing question, and searching for the answer has led us to simply exercise of a set of skills. That is just not enough. In fact, it is the fundamental problem at the root of our organizational dilemma. When an organization begins to exist first and foremost for the sake of a *telos*, its leaders come to embrace that cause in a deeply personal way. The *telos* must become their own, and so cause them to be its servants, not its masters.

Pathways to becoming a purposeful enterprise

As we continue this exploration, it may help to break down the different starting points and journeys that an organization might take toward becoming a purposeful enterprise. From what I've observed, there are five common paths:

Start-Up – Founder or Executive Led: **Leaders set up a new or young business to deliver on *telos* early on and build the brand and culture around their values and actions.**

Example: A few friends, frustrated by the high price of a product they believe should be universally available and the near-monopoly that keeps that price high, start a disruptive business. They launch Warby Parker and offer designer eyewear at a lower price while creating a sustainable and socially conscious busines. In telling the story of the company, they also point out that they believe "everyone has the right to see." And so for every pair of glasses sold, they partner with a nonprofit to provide a pair to someone in need and develop providers of basic optometry who offer their services in underserved areas. The *telos* was baked right in from day one.

Small/Medium Enterprise (SME) – Owner or Executive Led: Company leaders experience metanoia or undergo a regime change. They lead the discovery and activation of the company's *telos* and reshape the organization to implement it.

Example: The Ian Martin Group, a family-owned technical recruitment and project-staffing agency based in Toronto undergoes a leadership transition. Seeking to focus, grow, and preserve the ethos of the business, the new CEO and his team lead an ambitious, self-directed purpose-discovery effort. The aspiration they uncover – to connect people with meaningful work so that one day, the 20% of people who love their jobs will become 80%, and the world will be a different place – leads the company to launch Fitzii, a freemium software platform that matches people with jobs based on skills, personality, and culture.

The company meets comprehensive standards that measure their impact on employees, clients, community, and the environment, becoming a Certified B Corporation and a founding member of the B Corp movement in Canada.

Small/Medium Enterprise (SME) – Employee Led: Employee leaders, through personal conviction, are relentless in questioning their bosses and the company, pressing their sphere of influence to discover and activate the company's *telos*. Their efforts shape the culture and even the brand enough for the titular leaders to take notice and redirect the organization toward implementing or rediscovering purpose.

Example: A small grocery store chain in New England called MarketBasket fires its beloved CEO. Employees revolt and impel the board to reinstate him. The positive values the CEO stands for and the respectful, honest way he treats customers and employees become even more entrenched.

Corporation – Board or Executive Led: Leaders of a well-established business, either as a response to a personal conviction or as part of a regime change, lead the discovery and implementation of a *telos* and reshape the organization accordingly.

Example: CVS decides to end its tobacco sales in the United States. Their announcement is unambiguous: "Ending the sale of cigarettes and tobacco products at CVS Pharmacy is simply the right thing to do for the good of our customers and our company. The sale of tobacco products is inconsistent with our purpose – helping people on their path to better health." This reference to their purpose and difficult action to align with it represents a change of heart for the company, and CVS moves from providing what customers want to working to improve health outcomes. The company even rebrands itself as CVS Health in the process. This is CVS's corporate *telos* in action, a shift in intent, an adjustment to outward identity, and a change in business practice and actions in the marketplace.

Corporation – Employee Led: Employee leaders, out of personal conviction, are relentless in questioning their bosses and the company, pressing their sphere of influence to discover and activate the company's *telos*. Their efforts shape the culture and even the brand enough for the titular leaders to take notice and redirect the organization toward implementing or rediscovering purpose.

Example: An initiative that began as a small skunkworks funded with seed capital by the CEO catches fire among employees who have long been frustrated by their parent company's focus on shareholder value maximization. An emerging program to repurpose the business assets to innovatively create classroom learning about growing healthy food in marginalized urban communities wins scores of volunteers.

A grassroots movement takes hold in an otherwise cynical environment, and the challenge becomes structuring enough work, not finding enough volunteers. It begins to reshape the company, much to the confusion of the parent company – which is myopically focused on the capitalization value of the company.

An instructive failure and a dynamic catalyst for change

In the late 1980s, Kodak had an elevated opinion of its own power and greatness — a legacy of its founder and ownership, and confirmed, it seemed, by generations of success and strong market position. But all that disappeared in what seemed like a heartbeat.

On the surface, it was confounding. Kodak was packed with brilliance, its labs stuffed with technological treasures and digital wonders. This was, after all, the same collection of genius that invented digital photography. And yet, despite that pedigree and capability, Kodak was unable to free itself from the bondage of its own previous innovation — the alchemy of silver halide chemistry — which had revolutionized image capture and made Kodak the global leader in film and development technology.

What felled mighty Kodak was not Sony, Canon, or even Apple — fierce competitors though they were. Rather, Kodak was brought first to dismissal from the Dow Jones, and then eventually to its knees, not by its competitors but by its owners, the shareholders. Make no mistake: This was a suicide.

Those who desired a successful Kodak, measured by the traditional metrics of revenues and share price, are most culpable for the demise of their own prized asset. This was a company marked not by foolish managers but by foolish owners. Certainly, there were mistakes in management, but they were dwarfed by the crushing demand (in the form of regular and shrill insistence by the shareholders and their representatives — the Board of Directors) that Kodak should focus on film and not digital. At the precise moment when clear and long-term thinking was most needed, it was much more attractive to chase one more dollar from the existing (and immensely profitable) business than to risk a change in direction in order to succeed in a lower-margin business.

As you'll remember, *panarchy* teaches that over time, single-variable optimization destabilizes the system. The decision-makers at Kodak drove the company toward the addictive variable of profit, the only variable they cared to chase, and when the inevitable cliff appeared (it usually comes sooner than expected), they could not avoid it.

Some years ago, I wanted to try to understand the nature of addiction and how destructive patterns of behavior are replaced by more helpful choices. To do so, I reasoned, would help me understand the root of real organizational transformation, one person at a time. I was reading a book entitled *Addiction and Grace* by Gerald May and was enthralled by his deconstruction of habitual behavior patterns. I read on enthusiastically, anticipating at every turn that the pivotal moment of change and its genesis would soon be revealed. As this holy grail of insight hove into view, my expectation grew, and then there it was, the wise Dr. May's single cogent proposal.

When the harmful behavior pattern presented itself, the solution was "don't do it," and of the helpful behavior pattern, the corollary solution was "do it." That was it.

All the genius of his psychiatric training, all his knowledge about how behavior patterns change led to this one insight: Make a different choice in the moment of action. But if you think about it, it really is the hinge point of positive change. If Kodak's board had been able to free itself from the addictive comforts of a profitable past and a lucrative line of business long enough to make different choices at a few precise moments, would the company that invented the digital camera have retained the trust and imagination of customers in the exploding segment of image capture and produced other innovations that help people preserve their memories?

Of course, we'll never know what might have happened to Kodak. But the mere thought focuses us in on the simple yet profound truth that organizations change only when people do. We are the most dynamic catalyst of change.

If you continue making the same choices, chasing the same aspirations, and embodying the same things you have observed in the brand and culture of your organization, it certainly will not change. So if your organization is not yet a purposeful enterprise, but you desire it to recognize and embrace a telos, the best thing you can do is to recognize your unique capability to act, and to get to work instigating the purposeful enterprise to life.

A PURPOSEFUL ENTERPRISE STARTS WITH YOU

For generations, the system default for business has been profit maximization. We have tuned our companies into relentlessly effective economic engines with the solitary aim of accumulating wealth through value creation. For that reason, over the years, wholesale exploitation and inhumane behaviors of all sorts could simply be qualified as "good business" ... as long as the profits kept arriving. But we can no longer afford profit-only. With the economic and social challenges we face, today people are demanding a broader set of outcomes from companies than the singular variable of profit.

The complex system of business — which rests on a delicate set of commercial and capitalist principles and comprises shareholders, customers, employees, suppliers, regulators, auditors, and legislators — is entering a state of entropy. Companies must evolve in order to survive and thrive, and we must each do our part to help the system arrive at a healthier state.

Before we can begin, most of us will need to address a prior emotional response that could scuttle whatever hopes and plans we might have. Here's why: The conclusion that the system has to change produces feelings of powerlessness and insignificance.

In other words, we are still left with one burning question: Can we really change such a deeply entrenched default in such a complex system?

The answer is, "Yes." Although business is a highly complex system, it is not anonymous or uncontrollable — without our actions or input, it does not exist. We are not trapped in the Abilene Paradox — that group behavior where every member of a group chooses together an action that none would choose alone. Each of us who are employees, buyers, leaders, directors, investors, and voters has at least one point of influence in the system.

There are four habits we must embrace if this better way for business is to catch on:

> Demand Different Returns. In order to get full function from this incredible institution called "business," we will have to demand different returns from our companies than we have in the past. We must train their focus on a wider set of deliverables, a shift that will orient business in unfamiliar, and sometimes uncomfortable, ways. Discomfort is a consequence of change, and it is what we'll experience when we turn our businesses into purposeful enterprises that deliver for society. No other institutional form is as resilient and adaptive as business. Good businesses are hardwired for relevance, can turn on a dime, and have a long history of applying measurement to enhance performance. "What gets measured gets done," drones the mantra —
> so let's change the measures. Many businesses already are.

> Engage Personal Transformation. In order to manage this new kind of company, we will have to choose to behave and think differently. There is no such thing as business transformation without personal transformation. As has always been the case, personal shifts are the

fundamental movement of change. There is no substitute for a change of heart, no change management technique, no management theory that will do. Hearts and minds must change and at a deeply personal level.

Get Comfortable with Intensifying Uncertainty. Mass digital influence is here to stay, tastes seem to change more rapidly than ever, competition is fierce, and the pressure to innovate rapidly and successfully is increasing. The corporate boom and bust cycles seem to be tightening in the tech age (how many rapid declines can you name beyond Kodak, AOL, and Blackberry?). Decisions are becoming more complex and carry higher stakes. Fear is a given. Careful consideration, courage, conviction – and perhaps most of all, creativity – will be essential. Thankfully, some have already gone ahead with attempts to pierce this uncertainty and create a new future that is not just some utopian illusion, but a real alternative to the status quo.

Look to Spark the Multiplier Effect. What is necessary for these positive changes to come about is the multiplier effect that occurs when one person brings another along, spurring on another set of new choices. *Showing* new patterns of thinking and doing will always be a better teacher than *telling* about them.

Personally adopting these four habits will help you spur the creation of purposeful enterprises from your corner of the business landscape, whether you are a customer, a manager, or a CEO.

The truth is, bold actions like these four habits are what we must undertake if we are really going to change business for the better. But what causes us to gain clarity, see things differently, and ultimately step out in such bold action?

The answer quickly leads beyond what we do into the far more complex territory of who we are.

Metanoia: The root of all positive change

Most of us can look back and note times in life when our ideas and corresponding actions shifted trajectories. For Ebenezer Scrooge, it was a dreamlike spiritual experience that confronted him with reality. The religious term *conversion* also represents such a change, as do falling in love and the adoption of a cause through personal crisis or simple curiosity.

Whenever a person experiences a paradigm shift to a different level of reality, metanoia is what has occurred. It is what happens when a person puts away childish things. For instance, when a man stops treating his spouse in a way that mimics the behavior of his parents when he was a child, or when a woman quits treating that new colleague like she might have treated a new kid in the schoolyard.

Metanoia

A personal change of heart and mind that spurs behavior change.

All change begins with an awakening, and so this critical transformation of metanoia is the first thing that lifts the major barriers to change. The change of heart and mind leads to a change in behavior, and these changes almost always precede the living out of *telos*.

Organizations only change as individuals, especially those with influence, make different choices. The purposeful enterprise only happens one person, one choice, one metanoia at a time. Therefore, personal metanoia on a sufficient scale is an essential ingredient in a whole company's migration toward becoming a purposeful enterprise. It is a personal change of heart that spreads, and it has to start with someone, or else it doesn't happen.

The seven marks of metanoia

The experience of metanoia has seven distinct characteristics which can be summed up in this statement: We experience something (1) boundless and unexpected, (2) beyond reason, and (3) mysteriously compelling that sparks (4) nonconformity borne of conviction, a (5) deeper connection to others, a (6) fuller knowledge of our own story and identity, and a (7) vision of a better world.

Metanoia moves us to embrace something – a cause, a direction, or a new reality that is often much larger than we are, even BOUNDLESS. We are drawn beyond our previously understood limits, outside of our comfort zone and into an unexpected domain. As we step out (sometimes even to our own surprise) in that UNEXPECTED new direction, we become part of something larger that often yields a deeper sense of meaning and purpose.

While our minds are often rigorously engaged in reason, and thought may dominate the discovery of our new point of view after metanoia, our response may defy mere rationalism and take us BEYOND REASON in ways that are often intensely, deeply personal. It is not simply that we change our minds or even that they are persuaded to change, but rather that we ourselves are changed. For that reason, metanoia brings with it an energy that lifts us beyond the contingencies of our own resources, like the Newton's Cradle, whose five suspended metallic balls clicking back and forth seem to create their own energy. More powerful than any force of will we might generate, the change of heart and mind is MYSTERIOUSLY COMPELLING. As a colleague recently said to me, "I just cannot go back." Metanoia produces momentum greater than even our own desires, momentum that mysteriously propels our shift in attitude or action.

The simple phrase "a change of heart and mind" means metanoia always induces some kind of rejection of the status quo. For those who have experienced metanoia, to continue the status quo becomes intolerable, even impossible – and so NONCONFORMITY BORNE OF CONVICTION is inevitable. This usually manifests outwardly, as it may involve a change in factors such as priorities for action, relationships, or even whole career trajectories.

Such nonconformity does not result from a lack of fear — it arises from deep-seated conviction. At a much deeper, even subconscious level, metanoia may involve the rejection of long-ingrained patterns of thought, habit, or action that are enforced by factors like childhood experiences, adaptation to environments, or response to our own suffering.

Through metanoia, we are inevitably drawn into deeper relationships with others. People often speak of joining a movement — something they cannot manufacture alone — where they discover A DEEPER CONNECTION TO OTHERS that breaks down the myths of isolation and individualism and binds them not to things or abstractions, but to other people in unity — allies in a new cause that a "we" will take up together.

A change of heart and mind often brings a greater sense of self. We might express these sorts of discoveries with sentiments like "This is what I was born for!" We may consider ourselves to be self-made, but we are not. This becomes especially clear as our sense of self emerges from the complexities of our unique narrative and connection to others. Metanoia brings us to A FULLER KNOWLEDGE OF OUR OWN STORY AND IDENTITY. For this reason, this change of heart and mind is both desirable (for its transformative and positive qualities) and fearsome (for the personal consequences that usually result, which for the most part lie beyond our control).

As metanoia opens up horizons broader than those of our own creation and previous understanding, we discover opportunities and paths that were unexpected or even unimagined. We are opened to new possibilities through which our identity and capabilities are enlarged, perhaps beyond what we thought possible. With such enlargement of vision comes an invitation to bring more of ourselves than we may have even known existed with full commitment to a task or role. We find we have been granted A VISION OF A BETTER WORLD and are compelled to work for it.

We all have experienced metanoia at one time or another. Many of us may be able to reflect on our stories and locate with ease those remarkable and pivotal moments in our lives when everything changed, when we felt almost as if we had become a different person, or in fact, more fully ourselves. I think such expressions of life and depth and color tend to be the greatest means for change in what often feels like the mundane, black-and-white territory of business.

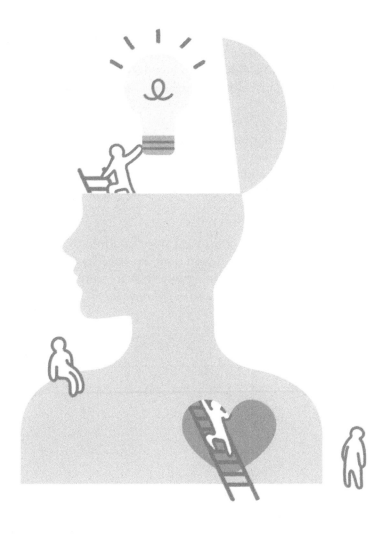

A few real-life examples of the effects of metanoia may help unpack this idea further:

- A world leader who ascended to the stratosphere of democracy leaves politics to become an advocate and chief spokesman in support of the controversial issue of climate change, a subject that had been a longtime focus of his personal and legislative agenda dating back to his college days, when he likely experienced metanoia related to the issue. Search for Al Gore.

- An economist and aspiring businessman defies conventional wisdom and lends his own money to impoverished entrepreneurs in Bangladesh, soon revolutionizing banking and poverty reduction efforts worldwide. Look up Muhammed Yunus and you'll probably find clues in his story that point to metanoia.

- An experienced management consultant steps out from the comfort of work he has become respected for and done for decades to begin a lengthy, costly and challenging endeavor in writing to share something he is seeing with others because it might help and encourage them. Actually … that's my story.

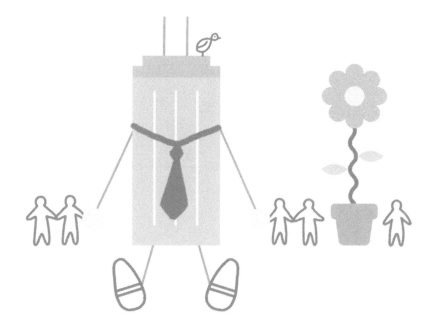

System change: A rising tide lifts all boats

System change begins with nonconformity. This requires unusual courage; not of fearlessness, but of conviction. Whether acting alone or as a group, choosing to bring about positive system change will at times feel like overturning the apple cart — an uncomfortable jolt followed by a certain mess! And yet, the accumulated impact of a change of heart and mind in one person after another will gradually begin to raise the standards for normal behavior. We must also be mindful when confronted by a new point of view or idea and remain humble enough to entertain its positive merits.

The seeds of positive system change are delicate and easily stifled. For instance, some years ago, a senior executive counseled a friend of mine that she "cared too much." Although he was likely not aware of it at the time, in giving this advice he also indicated that he was not yet ready to join her in caring more, thus stifling a positive change in an employee engagement program she had hoped to lead and signaling a definitive cultural identity (to "care less" perhaps?) at that particular firm. This resettled the organization into the same rut of mediocrity in which it remains. A small, simple sign from a seemingly harmless conversation that ended up speaking volumes.

When a metanoia occurs both personally and organizationally, it often sparks creativity and supplies an energy that lifts us beyond the limitations of our own resources and even our previous capabilities.

Look around. The signs of metanoia are everywhere. It's changing lives, but it's also changing the way the system of business works. It's clear: The purposeful enterprise starts with you, and metanoia is the seed of change.

CONCLUSION

In the study of change management, there are about as many models and theories as there are companies on which to practice. After some 30 years of coaching change in well-established businesses, I have become deeply skeptical of any short-term fixes like restructuring, reorganizing, or re-anything else. Habituated patterns of behavior — organizational or otherwise — do not yield easily to these traditional, blunt instruments of change.

We need only to examine our own habits and behavior changes to find evidence of that truth. The degree of difficulty in adopting a new personal behavior or giving up an old habit is the same as that encountered by any well-meaning effort to change a company, except that a while group of habits must be changed instead of just one.

The effort to make business better will require us to come to deep personal understanding of two virtues at the core of any meaningful change. This unique pairing is the final and most essential aid for our journey toward the purposeful enterprise, and it is composed of equal parts courage and humility – we might call it the *corporate twinity*.

For many years, shaped by the cultural celebration of success, we have tended to see humility as some kind of disability. Humility is not an attribute we tend to aspire to, because it seems hardly likely that a humble person would win an investment on *Dragons' Den* or *Shark Tank,* let alone become the CEO of a successful global corporation. As Lord Thomson of Fleet, one of the last of the newspaper barons, was once said to opine, "Humility, I've no use for it! Where would I be if I'd been humble?!" Traditionally, in Western culture, humility has been associated with weakness or a lack of self.

Yet, brash self-confidence was no help to the CEO who in the fall of 2015 raised the price of a simple but essential prescription drug from $13 to $750 per pill. He spent his much-coveted 15 minutes of fame blustering away, trying self-assuredly to quell the ire of thousands of vocal critics. Hardly a scrap of humility could be found in the character of this investment bulldog at the helm of a small drug company. His rhetoric failed miserably. Some months later, in what seemed to be a masterful stroke of comic justice, he was arrested for securities fraud. The man who has become known in the media as the "pharma-bro" and perhaps "most hated man in America" has certainly done some unwise and unseemly things, and he has been subject to a public flogging that he would not have faced just 10 years ago. Something has changed.

Within the very same week that this out-of-touch pharmaceutical CEO engaged in his series of self-centered strategic and PR blunders, rows and rows of people lined the streets just to glimpse the passing humble sedan of another organizational leader helming a vast organization with branches in virtually every town in the Western world and exploding growth elsewhere. He was on his way to Washington to preach the merits of the Golden Rule: Treat others as you would like them to treat you. When he arrived, we got to see the positive effects of humility on full display, for there is no doubt that his humility was a large part of the reason that he was greeted by the unanimous and thunderous applause of his ferociously divided audience: a joint session of the U.S. Congress. The Pope seems well aware that the habits of his life, the words from his mouth, and the meditations of his heart are on display for the world, and therefore may foment change for good. His humble and courageous leadership seems to be having just that effect.

Humility is the quality of rightly seeing one's place in context and in right relationship to others. Humility does not demand timidity but is a virtue that insists upon self-awareness, social intelligence, confidence, and service to others.

If we are able to transform this remarkable institution called business and harness its unparalleled capacity to do good, we will succeed because we place it as a servant of that good, not as an amoral agent of its own absorption. A business that sees itself in right relationship to its social context can only emerge when its people see themselves in right relationship to others. It is no longer adequate for business to own a space of pure commercial exploitation for its own (and its owners') sake.

We must put business to work in service to human need rather than human greed.

To serve demands humility, and business can only inherit this necessary virtue from leaders who embody it. The humble leader, as agent of change, may be a private or public person, CEO or financial analyst, corporate officer or co-op student.

The other, equally critical half of this corporate twinity is courage — the quality of doing what's right despite the personal cost. Courage does not demand heroics or stirring speeches or violent oppressors (à la William Wallace and other rebellious Scots my heritage may claim). Rather, like humility, it is a virtue that insists upon self-awareness, social intelligence, confidence, and service to others. It is the better known and more celebrated of these two essential attributes — and certainly the more attractive of the two in our postmodern and still highly individualistic age. Recently, a large tech company publicly cited courage as the reason they decided to alter the release of a popular product in order to make a new proprietary (and by many accounts suboptimal) piece of hardware essential for consumers to buy in order to use the legacy product. Do such self-serving actions really demonstrate courage? Apparently not, because the response of the masses was swift: reject the claim and scoff at the brand. Courage cannot simply be claimed — it must be demonstrated and conferred.

It takes courage to tell the boss that further cost rationalization will harm the customer, even though a bonus may well be contingent on the task.

It takes courage to declare a purpose, knowing full well that a critical mass of employees will hold you to account if you don't live up to it.

It takes courage to challenge a remarkably skilled employee who is a corrosive influence on other employees and the culture, even though he appears wildly successful on many fronts.

To the courageous, such action is self-evident. A given. The product of a conviction that difficulty and opposition simply cannot sway.

Today, we have the kind of businesses that we as consumers and employees have chosen. **While none of us will single-handedly counteract some of this form of capitalism's corrosive power, we can summon the courage to become a critical mass of both customers and employees who will change business for the better. The purposeful enterprise will only come about when this occurs.**

This change calls for each of us to be prepared to live courageously as people who align our buying behavior to our personal values, to live as employees who demand that the companies we work for pursue a *telos*, to live as leaders who reward behavior that delivers the *telos* and insist that the brand's reality match its promises. We must be executives who insist that owners create long-term benefits and not simply harvest financial gain, directors who set performance benchmarks that satisfy the *telos* and who are unwilling to capitulate to short-term interests, and regulators and inspectors who set standards that lead to long-term social benefits.

Turning business into an agent for good is possible only to the extent that each of us can see our own needs and wants in the context of others and act with humility and courage. If we do this more often, then together we can make business, and the world, a little better. For goodness' sake, we must!

KEY TAKEAWAYS

The End of Growth. We've designed business to do one thing and do it well: make money. But we have exceeded the world's capacity for continued wealth extraction. We've reached the end of the kind of growth to which we have been accustomed.

Act: Give up on bringing back business as it worked before. Instead, consider what "enough" or "natural market share" might consist of in your industry and how your business could be aimed at some kind of positive social impact.

Panarchy Rules. The system of business is subject to panarchy, a natural law governing complex systems. We have optimized for profit — a single variable chosen at the expense of all others — so much and so well that we have exceeded the system's capacity to deliver it. The law of panarchy will tip the system into a less stable state until balance is restored.

Act: Look beyond the surface of traditional business rules and see the bigger dynamic at work. Since profit alone can no longer be your primary goal, what good thing could your business do that would make the world a better place? Aim for that.

Reason Fails. The rise of rationalism applied to economics has made making money an irrefutable logic. But making money has its limits, and we need to recover means of justification for behavior other than simple economics.

Act: Recall the choices you have made that account for economic logic as well as other, possibly more important, criteria. You can apply that same thought pattern to your company and to your job.

Revenge of the Selfless Gene. Humans are a unique balance of a self that is defined by our uniqueness (*ipse*) and in the context of relationship with others (*idem*). Cultural preference for one or the other has oscillated throughout history. Today, it is swinging back toward *idem,* and that shift is mirrored in business.

Act: Locate companies that are ahead of the pack in finding identity in relationship with and in the context of others. This might look like a brand that is co-created and truly shared with people outside the company, or really seems to exist to serve a social good.

Meaning Matters Most. We have an innate desire to serve others, but business culture has blunted it. That is changing as more people are rediscovering meaning in life and business. Businesses, too, are exploring how they serve others and in ways that are surprisingly philosophical.

Act: Awaken your desire to make a difference for others. Act on it, and bring your business or employer along for the ride.

A Million Davids (Defeat Corporate Goliaths). Business in the 21st century has been shaped or given boundaries by three main voices: the market, regulators, and shareholder value. A fourth voice has grown and is louder than all before: regular people, amplified by social media and the Internet. Business is listening. It has to.

Act: Listen for the fourth voice and encourage others to hear what it is saying.

Fake Purpose. Purpose is everywhere these days, so much so that it seems like a fad, which makes it tempting for companies to manufacture a purpose and push it out. Purpose-washing will always pale next to authenticity.

Act: Examine your business and your life for purpose-washing and consider how you might turn a productized purpose into a deeply felt one.

New Wine Bursts Old Wine Skins. The business case for purpose is a cop-out. It reinforces the aim of the system to continue focusing on profit. What we need is the purpose case for business.

Act: Ask for the purpose case for business. Do the right thing for its own sake and not because rational economics says we might have something to gain from doing so.

Telos Inside. Each company has a unique purpose-for-others (its *telos*) that when discovered will reformulate the organization and unlock huge potential for positive impact.

Act: Look around you. There are businesses getting serious about social impact. There are nonprofits getting serious about economic viability. Ignore the old divisions.

Social Impact. Businesses are on their way to becoming the entities that address important social needs and human problems at every strata and on every scale.

Act: Help move corporations toward this end. Corporations will become the instruments and recipients of careful stewardship by owners and managers whose personal commitment to the telos of that organization is evident.

The Purposeful Enterprise. We know the core organizational building blocks of every purposeful enterprise: *telos* (a purpose-for-others), brand integrity that declares the *telos*, and an animating culture that proves the *telos*.

Act: Help build viable new models rather than waiting on some esteemed business journal to lay out a perfect plan. Purposeful enterprises will grow from experimentation.

Champion Change. The transformational levers that we can use to bring forth *telos* in purposeful enterprises are choices in strategy, aspiration in the culture, and embodiment in leaders.

Act: Either embody or nurture inspiring leadership that lives out the telos. Change is driven by those who choose it actively.

Transformed People Transform Companies. Systems change because people change them, not because of some arms-length strategy and culture technique that got implemented. Metanoia — an individual change of heart and mind — is the root of all positive change, and it comes from conviction and a mysteriously compelling sense of mission.

Act: Find two or three simple ways you can help bring about metanoia in those around you in life and business. Remember that purpose is personal, not professional.

A Personal Place. We are all actors and not casual observers. The corporate twinity of courage and humility will be essential.

Act: Reject cynicism. Don't wait for the time to be right. The right time is now. Bloom where you are planted.

NOTES, LINKS AND FURTHER READING

Introduction

11   "City Chief on Buyouts: 'We're Still Dancing.'" *The New York Times Dealbook,* July 10, 2007.

14   Lance H. Gunderson and C.S. Holling. *Panarchy: Understanding Transformations in Human and Natural Systems.* Island Press. 2nd Ed. 2002.

The failure of success (and how we got here)

21   Paul Ricoeur. *Oneself as Another.* University of Chicago Press, 1992.

21   Rene Descartes. *Discourse on the Method.* 1637.

21   John Locke. *Essay Concerning Human Understanding.* 1689.

21   Friedrich Nietzsche. *Thus Spoke Zarathustra.* 1883.

23   Adam Smith. *An Inquiry into the Nature and Causes of the Wealth of Nations.* 1776.

23   Alexis de Tocqueville. *Democracy in America.* 1840.

23   *Dartmouth College v. Woodward.* 17 U.S. 518. 1819.

25   *The Wolf of Wall Street.* Paramount Pictures, 2014.

25   "Even at the End, Ken Lay Didn't Get It." *The New York Times.* July 6, 2006.

26   World Meteorological Organization. "WMO confirms 2016 as hottest year on record, about 1.1°C above pre-industrial era." January 18, 2017.

28   Susan David. "Disengaged Employees? Do Something About It." *Harvard Business Review,* July 15, 2013.

28   World Health Organization. *Global Health Observatory Data.* "Urban population growth."

29   Lance H. Gunderson and C.S. Holling. *Panarchy: Understanding Transformations in Human and Natural Systems.* Island Press. 2nd Ed. 2002.

31   "City Chief on Buyouts: 'We're Still Dancing.'" *The New York Times Dealbook,* July 10, 2007.

32   "Coke, Pepsi dropping controversial 'BVO' from all drinks." *USA Today,* May 5, 2014.

33   Don Peppers and Martha Rogers. *Extreme Trust: Honesty as a Competitive Advantage.* Portfolio, 2012.

33   Deloitte. *Mind the gaps: The 2015 Deloitte Millennial Survey.* 2015.

33   Deloitte. *The Millennial Survey 2011.* 2011.

33   Deloitte. "Millennials want business to shift its purpose." 2016.

34   Pew Research Center. "Millennials Surpass Gen Xers as the Largest Generation in U.S. Labor Force." May 11, 2015.

34   Christine Elliot and William J. Reynolds. *Making it Millennial: Public policy and the next generation.* Deloitte University Press, 2014.

34   Pew Research Center. *Millennials in Adulthood.* March 7, 2014.

The failure of success – further reading

Malcolm Gladwell. *David and Goliath: Underdogs, Misfits, and the Art of Battling Giants.* Little, Brown and Company, 2013.

Malcolm Gladwell. *Outliers: The Story of Success.* Little, Brown and Company, 2008.

Malcolm Gladwell. *The Tipping Point: How Little Things Can Make a Big Difference.* Little, Brown and Company, 2000.

Paul Hawken. *The Ecology of Commerce.* Weidenfeld and Nicolson, 1993.

Purpose for business: A byproduct of unrest

38 "People don't buy what you do, they buy why you do it." is a central premise of Simon Sinek's popular book *Start with Why: How Great Leaders Inspire Everyone to Take Action*. Portfolio, 2011.

38 John Seifert, Worldwide Chairman and CEO of Ogilvy & Mather, has often said, "Authenticity is the new coin of the realm." I've also encountered a similar metaphor in the 2007 Arthur W. Page Society report entitled *The Authentic Enterprise*.

38 This quote about companies proactively protecting the interest of their customers is the central argument in Don Peppers and Martha Rogers' book *Extreme Trust: Honesty as a Competitive Advantage*. Portfolio, 2012.

38 Chris Malone and Susan T. Fiske. *The Human Brand: How we relate to people, products and companies*. Jossey-Bass, 2013.

39 https://thegiin.org/impact-investing/

39 http://www.kering.com/en/sustainability/epl

39 http://integratedreporting.org/wp-content/uploads/2011/09/IR-Discussion-Paper-2011_spreads.pdf

39 https://iris.thegiin.org/

40 https://www.bcorporation.net/what-are-b-corps

40 https://www.usgbc.org/leed

40 https://greenbusinessbureau.com/how-gbb-certification-works/

40 http://fortune.com/change-the-world/

40 https://ww2.pointsoflight.org/civic50/

40 http://www.corporateknights.com/reports/global-100/

41 *Harvard Business Review. The Purpose Case for Business*. Harvard Business School Publishing, 2015.

Purpose for business – further reading

David Jones. *Who Cares Wins: Why Good Business is Better Business*. Financial Times/Prentice Hall, 2012.

Doc Searls. *The Intention Economy: When Customers Take Charge*. Harvard Business Review Press, 2012.

Don Peppers and Martha Rogers. *The One to One Future: Building Relationships One Customer at a Time*. Crown Business, 1993.

Jim Collins and Morten T. Hansen. *Great By Choice: Uncertainty, Chaos and Luck — Why Some Thrive Despite Them All*. Harper Business, 2011.

Rajendra Sisodia, Jagdish N. Sheth, and David Wolfe. *Firms of Endearment: How World-Class Companies Profit from Passion and Purpose*. FT Press, 2007.

Ryan Honeyman. *The B Corp Handbook: How to Use Business as a Force for Good*. Berrett-Koehler Publishers, 2014.

"The One-for-one Business Model: Avoiding Unintended Consequences." *Knowledge@Wharton*. University of Pennsylvania, 16 February, 2015. http://knowledge.wharton.upenn.edu/article/one-one-business-model-social-impact-avoiding-unintended-consequences/

For goodness' sake: Business for telos

48   Michael Porter and Mark Kramer. "Creating Shared Value" *Harvard Business Review*. Jan/Feb 2011. https://hbr.org/2011/01/the-big-idea-creating-shared-value

48   http://sharedvalue.org/about-shared-value

49   http://unfccc.int/paris_agreement/items/9485.php

51   Quote is from a fascinating and wonderful TED Talk Ray Anderson (1934-2011) gave in 2009 called, "The Business Logic of Sustainability."

51   "In the Future, People Like Me Will Go to Jail," *Fortune Magazine*, May 24, 1999.

52   https://warbyparker.com/history

55   Lance H. Gunderson and C.S. Holling. *Panarchy: Understanding Transformations in Human and Natural Systems.* Island Press. 2nd Ed. 2002.

For goodness' sake: Business for telos – further reading

Aaron Hurst. *The Purpose Economy: How Your Desire for Impact, Personal Growth and Community Is Changing the World.* Elevate, 2014.

Dev Aujla and Billy Parrish. *Making Good: Finding Meaning, Money and Community in a Changing World.* Rodale Books, 2012.

John Argenti. *Your Organization: What Is It For?* McGraw-Hill, 1993.

John Mackey and Rajendra Sisodia. *Conscious Capitalism: Liberating the Heroic Spirit of Business.* Harvard Business Review Press, 2013.

Richard Branson. *Screw Business as Usual.* Portfolio, 2011.

Roger Martin. *Fixing the Game: Bubbles, Crashes, and What Capitalism Can Learn from the NFL.* Harvard Business Review Press, 2011.

The character of every purposeful enterprise

60   Daniel H. Pink. *Drive: The Surprising Truth About What Motivates Us.* Riverhead Books, 2009.

The character of every purposeful enterprise: further reading

Arthur W. Page Society. *The Authentic Enterprise,* 2007.

Burke & Litwin. "A Causal Model of Organizational Performance & Change." *Journal of Management,* Vol. 18, No. 3. 1992.

John Argenti. *Your Organization: What Is It For?* McGraw-Hill, 1993.

How to bring a purposeful enterprise to life

68   Burke & Litwin. "A Causal Model of Organizational Performance & Change." *Journal of Management,* Vol. 18, No. 3. 1992.

72   John P. Kotter. "Leading Change: Why Transformation Efforts Fail." *Harvard Business Review,* January 2007.

72   Edgar Schein. *Organizational Culture and Leadership.* 2nd ed. Jossey-Bass, 1992.

74   Rob Goffee and Gareth Jones. *Why Should Anyone Be Led by You?* Harvard Business Review Press, 2006.

77   https://warbyparker.com/history

77   http://www.ianmartin.com/about

78   Chris Malone. "Loyalty Lessons from a Supermarket Showdown." Fidelum Partners, November 2014.

78   "CVS Health's Marketing Chief on Turning the Pharmacy Brand into a Healthcare Player." *Adweek,* March 2016.

80   "Kodak's First Digital Moment" *NY Times,* August 12, 2015.

80   Lance H. Gunderson and C.S. Holling. *Panarchy: Understanding Transformations in Human and Natural Systems.* Island Press. 2nd Ed. 2002.

81   Gerald May. *Addiction and Grace: Love and Spirituality in the Healing of Addictions.* HarperOne, 2007.

How to bring a purposeful enterprise to life: further reading

Arthur W. Page Society. *The Authentic Enterprise,* 2007.

Arthur W. Page Society. *Building Belief: A New Model for Activating Corporate Character and Authentic Advocacy,* 2013.

John Argenti. *Your Organization: What Is It For?* McGraw-Hill, 1993.

Patrick Lencioni. *The Advantage: Why Organizational Health Trumps Everything Else in Business.* Jossey-Bass, 2012

Seth Godin. *All Marketers are Liars: The Power of Telling Authentic Stories in a Low-Trust World.* Penguin, 2005.

Spencer Johnson, MD. Who Moved My Cheese? Putnam, 1998.

Stephan H. Haeckel. *Adaptive Enterprise: Creating and Leading Sense-and-Respond Organizations.* Harvard Business Review Press, 1999.

Terry O'Reilly. *This I Know: Marketing Lessons from Under the Influence.* Alfred A. Knopf, 2017.

A purposeful enterprise starts with you

83   Lance H. Gunderson and C.S. Holling. *Panarchy: Understanding Transformations in Human and Natural Systems.* Island Press. 2nd Ed. 2002.

87   Newton's cradle: http://gph.is/H3xNmP

90   Melinda Henneberger. "On Campus Torn by 60s, Agonizing over the Path." *The New York Times,* June 21, 2000.

90   Muhammad Yunus: Changing the world one small step at a time: https://youtu.be/hXeHo8wOL9o

A purposeful enterprise starts with you: further reading

Al Etmanski. *Impact: Six Patterns to Spread Your Social Innovation.* Orwell Cove, 2015.

Charles Handy. *The Empty Raincoat: Making Sense of the Future.* Hutchinson, 1994.

C. Otto Scharmer. *Theory U: Leading from the Future as It Emerges.* Society for Organizational Learning, 2007.

Daniel Goleman. *Emotional Intelligence: Why It Can Matter More Than IQ.* Bloomsbury Publishing PLC, 1995.

Harry Kraemer. *From Values to Action: The Four Principles of Values-Based Leadership.* Jossey-Bass, 2011.

John P. Kotter. *The Heart of Change: Real-Life Stories of How People Change Their Organizations.* Harvard Business Review Press, 2002.

Kim Scott. *Radical Candor: Be a Kick-Ass Boss Without Losing Your Humanity.* St. Martin's Press, 2017.

Margaret J. Wheatley. *Finding Our Way: Leadership for an Uncertain Time.* Berrett-Koehler, 2005.

Max De Pree. *Leadership Jazz.* Currency Doubleday, 1992.

Nancy Duarte and Patti Sanchez. *Illuminate: Ignite Change Through Speeches, Stories, Ceremonies, and Symbols.* Portfolio, 2016.

Patrick Lencioni. *The Five Dysfunctions of a Team: A Leadership Fable.* Jossey-Bass, 2002.

Roger Martin. *The Opposable Mind: How Successful Leaders Win Through Integrative Thinking.* Harvard Business Review Press, 2007.

Steve Farber. *Greater Than Yourself: The Ultimate Lesson of True Leadership.* Doubleday, 2009.

Seth Godin. *What to Do When It's Your Turn (and It's Always Your Turn).* Domino Project, 2014.

Conclusion

94   "Who is Martin Shkreli? A timeline." *CNNMoney*, December 18, 2015. http://money.cnn.com/2015/12/18/news/companies/martin-shkreli/index.html

94   "Pope Francis electrifies Congress with speech laying out bold vision for US." *The Guardian*, September 24, 2015. https://www.theguardian.com/world/2015/sep/24/pope-francis-congress-speech

Thanks

This book, like the proverbial 1000-mile journey, began with a simple first step — a sense that there was something that needed to be said. My friend Pierre, a CMO, encouraged the first hesitant steps that were supported by Miles Young, then CEO of Ogilvy & Mather. Soon, editor Jeremy Katz brought his passion and expertise and has remained faithful throughout. John Seifert, who became CEO of Ogilvy & Mather in 2016, has been always supportive and given me important work to do. Betsy Stark offered her journalistic rigor to sharpen the message. I am deeply grateful for the invaluable help provided by Ogilvy at so many points along this publishing journey.

Along the way, the encouragement of a longtime mentor and friend, Joe DiStefano, was invaluable. The early support of Rob, John, Wendy, Keith, and Eric, as well as the ongoing friendship of Andy and archetypal reader Katie, all made the journey lighter and worthwhile.

Later, copy editors Rob and Gail produced immense improvement to the text with thoughtful, challenging engagement, and Lucia brought the visual storytelling to life with her keen eye and creativity. There are many others to whom I am grateful, people who came along at precise moments when encouragement and a spike of courage were needed to keep going, and their words and actions helped provide it. Thank you.

So many clients opened doors to opportunities for discovery over the years. And my beloved wife and partner, Jeannie, offered the encouragement to explore what lay behind them despite the endless travel and long absences, not to mention numerous dark periods without inspiration, which she patiently endured with proffered hope.

This book stands upon the shoulders of my own father's life's work. Jim Houston has been (and continues to be) an endless source of insight and wisdom, and has provided a profound grounding that shaped me and my thinking beyond what I can recognize. It is his gift to me for life.

But no one deserves more credit than my colleague, partner, and coauthor in it all, Jordan Pinches, through whose youthful optimism and diligent, often painstaking work this book has come into being. But for Jordan, it would not exist, and for his person and his efforts, I am deeply grateful.

About the Author

Chris Houston is a biologist, management consultant, farmer, and grandfather whose life's work and calling have been to come alongside and walk with leaders, most often of businesses, as they navigate changes in and to their organizations. He's been at it for nearly 30 years, loves the work, and struggles with the peripatetic life it requires — but can't help looking for the next place to contribute, encourage, cajole, or create. As a client once said, "you sell the 'hard stuff' to earn the right to do the 'soft stuff.'" The "hard stuff" is strategy; the "soft stuff" is leadership, and the essential hybrid of sound thinking and right acting.

His clients span industries, continents, and sizes, from start-ups to global businesses, in North America and Europe, B2Cs and B2Bs. The work comes through a web of relationships and personal encounters. There have been some memorable failures, but fortunately, more successes have yielded the kaleidoscope of insights that are woven into the fabric of *For Goodness' Sake* like the threads of a carpet — each distinct, yet together forming a pattern of meaning.

When not in a client's office or on a plane, Chris can be found on his farm outside Toronto, with his wife Jeannie, or enjoying their growing family.

Chris began his career in business with his MBA (Gold Medalist) from The University of Western Ontario's Ivey School of Business in London, Ontario, in 1987. He then went on to join the General Management practice in the Toronto office of Woods Gordon, the Canadian consulting affiliate of what was then Arthur Young International and is now EY. Soon, however, Chris realized that his skills were better deployed in a boutique business model, and after a short stop in Change Lab International, he set out with colleague Morrey Ewing, and later on his own in the Change Alliance. It is in the independence and vulnerability of the sole practitioner that Chris has found his true calling — to be a servant of business leaders and their organizations.

Chris can be reached through www.telosity.net or through houston@changealliance.com.

Notes:

CPSIA information can be obtained
at www.ICGtesting.com
Printed in the USA
LVOW05s1132180917
548911LV00010B/4/P